Seasons
of the Wild

CHAPTERS PUBLISHING LTD., SHELBURNE, VERMONT 05482

Also by Sy Montgomery
Spell of the Tiger
Walking with the Great Apes

Material in this book originally appeared in slightly different form in *The Boston Globe*.

Published by
Chapters Publishing Ltd.
2031 Shelburne Road
Shelburne, Vermont 05482

Library of Congress Cataloging-in-Publication Data

Montgomery, Sy.
    Seasons of the wild: a year of nature's magic and mysteries / by Sy Montgomery; with a
foreword by Elizabeth Marshall Thomas; illustrated by Rodica Prato.
            p.   cm. — (The Curious naturalist series)
    Includes bibliographical references (p.) and index.
    ISBN 1-881527-90-5 (softcover)
    1. Natural history—United States. 2. Nature—United States. 3. Seasons—United States.
I. Title. II. Series.
    QH104.M66 1995
    508.73—dc20   95-22586

Trade distribution in the U.S. by Firefly Books (U.S.) Inc.
P.O. Box 1338 • Ellicott Station • Buffalo, NY 14205

Trade distribution in Canada by Firefly Books Ltd.
250 Sparks Avenue • Willowdale, Ontario • Canada M2H 2S4

Printed and bound in Canada by
Friesen Printers
Altona, Manitoba

Designed by Eugenie Seidenberg Delaney
Cover illustration by Rodica Prato

Yet again, to Dr. A.B. Millmoss

ACKNOWLEDGMENTS

THE ESSAYS IN THIS BOOK are constructed from a series of wonderings: What do robins do after dark? Who left those claw marks on the apple tree? Where are a jellyfish's lips? Why are pinecones growing on that willow? Which half of the worm is the front?

In the course of exploring these questions, I've had the pleasure of consulting a number of fellow nature lovers: children, scientists, poets, artists, philosophers, teachers, parents. Thanks to them, I can pass on to you the recipe for blackfly drool, the name brand of the favorite snack crackers of blue jays, and what to do if you want to get a katydid to answer you. To all who are quoted in these pages, I extend my thanks.

The sharp eyes and ears of many observers helped gather the information presented in this book. In particular, I am grateful to Eleanor Briggs, Kate and Jane Cabot, David Carroll, Ed and Lennie Duensing, Richard Estes, Lawrence Kilham, John Kulish, Farley Mowat, Roger Tory Peterson, Elizabeth Marshall Thomas and Rick and Wendy Van de Poll. Through their books, correspondence or presence, they have served as my walking partners, literal or metaphorical, while exploring the seasons of the wild.

To my husband, Howard Mansfield, my thanks for your love and tolerance. For all the spiders and moths and ants in our house I refuse to kill, blame my hero, E.O. Wilson, who counsels, "Be careful of little lives." With Tess, our border collie, my long-legged spouse has lead me on many a walk, so just about everything I've seen with them, let the record show, they saw first.

Christopher Hogwood, our 600-pound pig, isn't much of a walking partner, but for his excellent rooting abilities I thank him for providing useful assistance in researching the chapter on earthworms. He would have been more help if he hadn't eaten them, though.

I am grateful to the staff of a number of institutions for unearthing other resources. For locating experts, books and scientific reports, I acknowledge assistance from the Audubon Societies of New Hampshire, Massachusetts and Maine; Antioch/New England Graduate School; Cornell University's Laboratory of Ornithology; the Hancock Town Library; the Harris Center for Conservation Education; Harvard University's Museum of Comparative Zoology; the Peterborough Town Library; and New England Wild Flower Society.

A number of editors—none of whom, to their credit, will feel slighted by appearing in these acknowledgments after a pig—deserve recognition as well. Nils Bruzelius and Kathy Everly, the sensible and knowledgeable Health and Science editors of *The Boston Globe*, invited me to invent and write the column "Nature Journal," from which the chapters of this book are taken. For gathering these essays together, I thank my friends Sandy Taylor and Barry Estabrook, excellent editors both.

Most of all, I am indebted to the animals, plants, fungi, phenomena and landscapes depicted in these essays. It is with full confidence that they will speak with equal eloquence to all those who approach attentively that I have written this book. And, while few wild creatures have much use for literature, I do hope that at least book lice, and perhaps certain fungi, may also enjoy these pages.

CONTENTS

FOREWORD

Elizabeth Marshall Thomas

CONSIDERING THE IMPORTANCE of the natural world, it's surprising that most people know so very little about it. Yet our ignorance is a fairly recent development in the history of our species. In Paleolithic times, when we were hunter-gatherers, we surely knew a lot more—we had to.

It was once my great privilege to live among the Ju/wa Bushmen, the hunter-gatherers of the Kalahari Desert. These people understand their world in a way that even the naturalists and the scientists of our world cannot emulate. Among the Bushmen, almost everybody over the age of 12 recognized about the same number of species of plants and animals as botanists and zoologists recognize, but the Bushmen knew more than the scientists about the nutritive and medicinal properties of the plants and had great insight into the habits and behaviors of the animals. In short, they knew what everything was, and also what everything did. Also, most people could forecast the weather, were very creditable astronomers, and had much geological information especially as it pertained to the whereabouts of water.

A climax in knowledge of the natural world was their discovery of arrow poison. In the Kalahari are many thousands of kinds of beetles, of which one, a species of *Diamphidia,* is deadly poisonous in its pupa state. But the poison is only toxic when injected into the bloodstream, not when eaten, and the pupae are only found at the depth of about three feet in the sandy earth among the roots of marula trees. The grubs hatch from their eggs on the leaves of the tree, but vanish almost immediately as they burrow under the bark. When they emerge from the tree underground to pupate, they remain almost invisible, since they make their pupa casings from the surrounding sand so that the casings look like tiny lumps of the already lumpy earth. You can dig up any number of them by accident and never notice what they are. How the Bushmen found these grubs at all, let alone found that they contain a poison that is lethal when injected is hard to imagine, especially since eating the grubs allegedly doesn't even make you sick. Suffice it to say that the chances of stumbling onto such a phenomenon by accident are almost zero—such finds are made only by people who examine their world in every detail.

With the development of agriculture, and later, of industrial society, our familiarity with the natural world diminished. It wasn't entirely lost, but got deferred to certain specialists for interpretation—mainly scientists, but also writers, painters, photographers and the like. Interestingly enough, the plain observation that served us all so well when we were hunter-gatherers is now seldom valued as highly as a professional interpretation. The storms that rage through some of the plays of Shakespeare reflect the emotions of the characters and so become literature of high degree, more valued than a down-to-earth weather report could ever be. A book about a sperm whale, even if written by Melville, would never be accorded the status of *Moby Dick,* in which the whale is not only a whale but a catalyst for important human activity, a force of nature and a symbol of something or other—evil, if I remember right.

We have delegated the natural world to specialists, and we look to specialists for guidance—even for the language we use when discussing it. In an effort to emulate scientists, to seem proper, correct, scientific, unsentimental, to avoid the appearance of anthropomorphization, many of us feel compelled to discuss animals, say, in as flat and bloodless a manner as possible. Hence animals don't eat, they utilize food resources. They don't get angry or defensive, they exhibit agonistic behavior. They often don't have names, just numbers, and sometimes they aren't even considered as entire organisms—not when population densities are expressed in fractions, resulting in such unlikely statistics as 0.3 mountain lions per square kilometer. And finally, animals don't have gender. Supercorrect proponents of science-speak insist on calling animals "it," perhaps in fear readers would get all mushy about them if stimulated by even this tiny dram of personal information. The author of this very book, Sy Montgomery, was once criticized by an editor for using the pronoun "she" when referring to a crane. The editor tried to insist that Sy call the crane "it," even though the article was about an egg that she, the crane, had laid. On another occasion, Sy wrote about a snow leopard, calling him "shy and secretive." This too met the wrath of an editor. "Shy, perhaps," the editor said. "But secretive? Can we really say that a snow leopard has secrets?"

The answer, of course, is yes. Snow leopards, like all cats, keep many secrets from human beings and also from each other, including the location of nesting sites and the whereabouts of leftover food. The most important secret kept by snow leopards, however, is usually their presence, which for obvious reasons they keep from our kind in any way they can. However, the concept of secretiveness implies intent. That the animal should have intent seems perilously close to humanization. Better to treat the animal as a machine, and omit reference to such things as secrets.

Sadly, our inexperience combined with our neoscientific approach to the natural world has lead us far from many of the greater truths that hunter-gatherers see. We need people like Sy Montgomery to remember these truths, to remind us that the natural world is rich and fascinating, that we are not alien to it but are entirely capable of knowing it in all its wonder. She sees the natural world as a hunter-gatherer might see it, in all its splendid detail.

INTRODUCTION

WRITING ABOUT NATURE has its hazards. Researching other books, I've been chased by an angry silverback gorilla in Zaire, bitten by safari ants in Rwanda, robbed by an orangutan in Borneo (who then chewed up the interview tapes she had stolen from my backpack) and hunted by a tiger in India. I got dengue fever in Singapore and dysentery in Bangladesh. In Costa Rica, I was bitten on the finger by a vampire bat. (I richly deserved it—and I was wearing gloves.)

This book, I confess, was a piece of cake.

North America is great. For one thing, my husband's here. For another, it's ideal for exploring the natural world. You don't need a lot of shots, snakes don't crawl into your bed, poisonous caterpillars don't drop out of the sky, and as a rule, the trees don't exude toxic sap—yet here you can find landscapes and creatures as strange and mysterious as in any jungle.

Beneath your porch, creatures with their skeletons on their outsides and their ears on their knees are singing with their wings. Just outside your door, predators with 28,000 lenses in each eye are scarfing down prey, fighting off rivals and making love by flying around with their abdomens stuck to someone else's neck.

These are animals every child has watched—crickets and dragonflies. Turn your attention to the nearest tree, and you're likely to see members of utterly separate kingdoms making war, taking slaves, forming partnerships and chemically co-opting one another. Venture just a bit further afield, and more wonders await: in bogs, you'll find plants that eat animals; at the shore, animals who get on fine without heads; in your local stream, the most precious metal on Earth.

Without even leaving your house, though, just looking out your window, you may find flying squirrels flitting through the dark like furry Frisbees, bears fossicking through car trunks, cougars making a comeback, or even spot a wandering wallaby. (No kidding.)

Our lives are surrounded by ordinary miracles, everyday mysteries. To find them, all you need to do is indulge your senses. Follow the scent of the earth outdoors on a cool, wet morning in spring. On a hot August afternoon, go down to the local pond and watch dragonfly larvae crawl out of their skins. On a still December night, let the moonlight call you outdoors to listen to the wind sigh in the pines.

In other words, be a hedonist. Look out the window, find something wonderful, turn off whatever screen you're watching and go outside. You are certain to discover something wholly unexpected. The more you watch, the deeper the natural world will draw you into its mystery and magic.

Autumn

September's Insect Chorus

&❧

N HIS POEM "CONVERSATIONAL INSECTS," H.I. Phillips has a confession to make: "I long to interview the little Insects, / And get the drift of what they're driving at: / To chat with Wasps and Crickets / In bushes, trees and thickets / And understand the language of the Gnat."

If you share this poet's sensibilities, now is the time for your longing to be fulfilled. Though often overshadowed by the month's changing leaves and migrating birds, September is, in some circles anyway, renowned for the sweetness of its insect voices.

Now, as summer ripens into autumn, birdsong gives way to bug-song—providing, according to University of Massachusetts entomologist Vincent Dethier, "an extraordinary coda to the summer symphony."

Their songs tell of longing and pursuit, rivalry and battle: If the song of the autumn field cricket suddenly becomes louder, more rapid and higher pitched, he's located a lady and is calling to her. If his calls soften, she has come to him and is ready to mate. (Unlike grasshoppers, the female usually mounts the male.) If he encounters a rival, he chirps more loudly and the chirps get longer and less rhythmic—and a vicious battle may ensue. (So vicious that cricket fights were the entertainment extravaganzas of the Sung Dynasty of China in 900 A.D. The victors earned the title *shou lip*—"conquering cricket"—and were ceremoniously buried in little silver caskets when they died of old age.)

Some songs convey information people can use: because the insect's metabolism speeds up with the heat, the hotter the weather, the faster the chirping. The male snowy tree cricket, which begins singing in September and continues until the killing frost, tracks temperatures so accurately that in 1897, Tufts University professor A.E. Dolbear developed a measurement formula accurate to within 1 degree F: count the number of chirps in 15 seconds and add 39.

And there are songs with X-rated lyrics of which Tipper Gore would disapprove. Some species of grasshoppers, for instance, explicitly announce the moment of copulation with a distinct, sharp noise just before the male leaps onto the back of the female—a sound that one entomologist interprets as the orthopteran equivalent of "Oh, boy!" and terms "the shout of triumph."

The fall songs of these hopping insects are among the most lovely and lyrical sounds of the natural world. In Africa, the songs of crickets are said to have magic powers. Henry David Thoreau described the song of one species as "a slumberous breathing," an "intenser dream." Nathaniel Hawthorne, describing the autumn music of the snowy tree cricket, wrote: "If moonlight could be heard, it would sound like that."

Yet it is not always easy for people to tune in to the songs of insects. To aid in that endeavor, Dethier, whose parents were pianists and whose uncle played the violin, wrote *Crickets and Katydids, Concerts and Solos*, published by Harvard University Press in 1992. "We, who are preeminently creatures of vision, instinctively appreciate most the world of light," he writes. "We must learn to savor the full range of nature's world of sound." How? "Listen for silence," he advised over the phone. "Then you hear them."

If it takes some effort to listen for insect song, it is because, of course, the songs are not meant for us; they are meant for alien creatures who wear their skeletons on their outsides and whose ears are on their elbows. (Members of the grasshopper family, including crickets, locusts and katydids, hear with small disks near one of the front leg joints.) And these songs are perfect for their purposes.

Over the relatively long distances that these little animals must travel to find one another, looks mean nothing; songs call out the identity of the musician. For this reason, entomologists can some-times better classify them by their songs than by their appearance.

The songs of the grasshopper family are not sung, but fiddled. The sounds are produced with wings that function as "something between a string and a percussion instrument," as Dethier describes it—like a violinist playing pizzicato. The major sound-producing structure is a big wing vein that bears dozens, sometimes hundreds, of tiny ridges, like a file.

This file moves against a scraper—a hardened portion of the inner wing margin. A singing cricket rubs the file of one wing over the scraper of the other wing, while vibrating the wing membrane. You can often tell the male by his larger wings. The females are much quieter, often entirely silent.

Most crickets are right-winged: the "file" of the right wing is played upon by the scraper of the left. Each wing, though, has a scraper, and if you reverse the wing, a prank that entomologists play in the name of science, the cricket can sing with the left wing, but about as gracelessly as a right-handed person can write with the left hand. (But if the switch is made while the cricket is young, one researcher found, the cricket can still become a virtuoso.) Katy-dids, on the other hand, are left-winged.

Most autumn-singing insects prefer to sing on warm mornings, afternoons and early evenings. But if you listen carefully, you may be able to hear somebody or another singing almost any time. The greenish yellow marsh meadow locust prefers to sing on hot, quiet forenoons, from moist ditches and grassy banks. At night, in areas that have been spared aerial spraying, listen for the katydids. They'll be squawking from the same lindens, elms and maples where cicadas sang during the daytime in the summer.

If you talk to a katydid, it will answer you. Make a two-syllable sound, it responds in kind; utter three syllables, it responds with three. Dethier's katydids did not seem able to count beyond four. But Dr. Richard Alexander of Ohio State University reports that in the southern United States, a genius species of katydid thrives that can "count" up to six.

Neither Land Nor Water

The In-Between Realm of the Bog

&

THE BOARD PATH leads through what at first looks like a forest surrounding any wetland: red maple, cinnamon fern, royal fern, thickets of blueberry and huckleberry alive with the brightest early colors of autumn. But as you continue along the path, the trees get shorter and smaller. And finally, at a bend, a vista opens that takes your breath away: a meadow of garnet-red sphagnum moss, teal-colored bog rosemary, round white tufts of cotton grass atop tall slender stems, and the occasional struggling, bonsai-like black spruce. As autumn advances, the deciduous needles of the tamarack will yellow, and the moss-meadow will be circled in a halo of gold.

On a late September day, when crickets sing and kestrels soar, there could be no more beautiful spot on Earth than a bog.

Yet this is also the sort of place Sir Arthur Conan Doyle described as a "dark, quivering mire." Because of its bog, "the very name of Smith's Pond caused a shudder to run through the women of the neighborhood," Hopkinton, New Hampshire, resident Richard Gilman recalled in 1930. Bogs have literally swallowed up livestock. If there is no board walkway, you can sink through the carpet of sphagnum moss, in Doyle's words, "as if some malignant hand was tugging down into those obscene depths."

A bog is a sort of netherworld, evoking at once a reverent calm and a quaking fear. A bog is neither land nor water, but, as Vermont

State Naturalist Charles Johnson calls it, "a realm in between."

Bogs blur the boundaries between land and water, living and dead, plants and animals. The plants seem visibly to move, like animals: craggy branches of shrubs and trees seem posed like dancers; mosses and heaths creep across ground and water like snakes. Plants even take up meat eating here. At least two types of carnivorous plants thrive in bogs—the red-veined, green-spathed pitcher plant, which drowns its victims, and the tiny sundews, which snare them on droplets of sticky, spine-borne goo.

North America hosts many tens of thousands of bogs, and each is different. Some feature open water. Some are jammed with springtime orchids. Some are used to grow Thanksgiving cranberries. Some bogs—those nourished by trickles of flowing freshwater—are technically fens (though most of these places are named bogs anyway). Several, thanks to the ministrations of town conservation commissions, state parks and organizations like The Nature Conservancy, sport board walkways. These are the safest to visit, for both you and the bog.

All bogs share common characteristics: All have fibrous, peaty soils, made of barely decomposed dead plants and animals. All have standing, acidic water. But perhaps the most powerful defining feature of a bog is one you cannot see. "A bog has a strange, mystical feeling," says David Carroll, author of *The Year of the Turtle* and *Trout Reflections.* Carroll is still exploring bogs to do research for the third book in his "wet-sneaker trilogy," *Swampwalker's Journal.* "When I'm in a wild bog," he says, "even the wind sounds different."

Naturalist Johnson has felt it, too, in the first bog he visited as a child. "The place seemed to throb with deep energy," he writes in *Bogs of the Northeast.* "Some strange gods," he concludes, "have to be living there."

Northern Europe's ancient peoples apparently agreed. Scientists have retrieved from these bogs the bodies of Iron and Bronze Age people who lived between 1500 and 500 B.C. Some experts, notably Danish author and researcher Peter Glob, theorize that bogs were considered sacred to the Earth goddess Nerthus. These people

THE SPHAGNUM MOSS CARPET OF A BOG
CONCEALS A DEEP NETHERWORLD: BOGS HAVE
LITERALLY SWALLOWED UP LIVESTOCK.

may have been offered as sacrifices to her. The bogs' waters have pre-served the bodies, earning the victims a sort of immortality.

In the stillness of a bog, time itself seems arrested. "Even before I researched the kind of time involved in building a bog," says swampwalker Carroll, "I could feel a strange sense of time here." Time does not fly in a bog; time accumulates, like peat.

Peat forms very slowly: the upper 20 inches in the hollows of cer-tain bogs may take more than 2,000 years to accumulate. The peats themselves form "archives of history," in the words of one scientist. In the pollen and leaves, sedges and moss preserved in each bog, scientists with microscopes can read its life history.

Some bogs (including most of the best-known in New England) began as "kettleholes," deep basins carved by glaciers. What's most important in forming a bog, though, is standing water with little or no inflow or outflow. Only in such waters will peat form and sculpt the landscape of a bog.

Here, only plants that can tolerate nutrient-poor, oxygen-poor, acidic conditions survive. A floating mat of sedges, mosses and shrubs congeals across the water. As the mat thickens, it may support trees: red maple and white cedar at some sites, tamarack and black spruce at others. Look around. The plants surrounding you, Car-roll says, represent "a 10,000-year drama caught in a freeze frame."

Although land around a bog often teems with animals, living conditions in the bog itself may be too harsh to support even fish. This is primarily a plant realm.

In a bog, more than anywhere else, "you get more of a sense of plants as living organisms, as individuals," Carroll explains. "Look," he says, pointing to a stunted, lichen-crusted tamarack at Philbrick Cricenti Bog in New London, New Hampshire. Its trunk, gnarled and twisted like a tree on a Chinese scroll, is barely over two inches thick at its base, yet could be more than a century old. "Every branch, every lichen, every shadow on it, every shadow it casts," says Car-roll, "is perfect."

Pods

Blueprints for Immortality

ॐ

BLINDED BY THE BLAZE of autumn's foliage, we often miss what is, from the plant's point of view, its most spectacular efforts. After all, a plant's crowning achievement is neither its youthful flowers nor autumn leaves, but its blueprints for immortality: fruit, pods and seed heads. And long after autumn's brilliant leaves have been raked away, these structures will continue to offer a harvest of strange and beautiful forms.

"Our appetites have commonly confined our views of ripeness . . . to the fruits we eat," Thoreau wrote in his journal in October of 1858, "and we are wont to forget that an immense harvest which we do not eat, hardly use at all, is annually ripened by nature . . . fruits which address our taste for beauty alone."

Fruits, pods and seeds offer stunning colors, fantastic shapes: some are shaped like Japanese lanterns; others look like space capsules from Mars; one tall, puffy pod looks like the fanciful common name for this lily: Turk's cap.

You'll find much of this wild harvest worthy of your favorite vase. "To me, the empty seed container—the pod—is another of nature's works of art, as beautiful as the flower and as unique in its own form," Wisconsin watercolorist Jane Embertson believes. So taken was she with this often-overlooked beauty that she wrote a guide to using berries, seeds and pods in floral arrangements, entitled *Pods: Wildflowers and Weeds in Their Final Beauty.*

Asters' fuzzy tufts hold little round clusters of silky seed heads, which can be used in arrangements as you would baby's breath. Blue bead lily's beautiful deep blue, round berries branch out in a starburst pattern from the top of the leafless stalk and make stunning accents. Common milkweed's warty pods erupt with feathery parachutes of seeds, leaving soft, pale orange tongues clinging to silky yellow exteriors.

Many of these shapes and colors would grace gardens as well as wild places—but, notes Heather McCargo, New England Wild Flower Society's plant propagator, "most gardeners hack everything back after it blooms."

So, also, we miss many grasses' graceful seed heads: wild oats, for instance, sport clusters of flattened chevrons on chartreuse stems; Gray's sedge grows an astonishing mace-shaped seed head an inch across. "But we don't see them," says McCargo, "because we mow everything in sight." (Fortunately, at the Society's Garden in the Woods in Framingham, Massachusetts, they don't; so there, as well as in your local woods, fields and swamps, you can see many of these pods, fruits and nuts still on the plant.)

All of these structures are vehicles for seeds. A look at their shapes foretells their travels: milkweeds' parachutes and maples' whirligig pods are designed to ride the wind. Well-named sticktights and burdock burrs hitchhike on fur and clothing. Lantern- or bladder-shaped pods of wetland species like water chestnut are designed to float like buoys on trips downstream. A few are entirely self-propelled: jewelweed's seeds literally shoot off the plant if you brush against it. (Peel away the thin green pod for a tasty walnut-flavored field snack.)

Even the taste and beauty of berries are pure packaging designed to move the merchandise. Many fruits' first job is to catch attention: red gooseberries show up against green leaves; bright red stems offset purple elderberries; and white fruits, like those of creeping snowberry, contrast with dark stems or a solid background of moss or dead leaves. Enticed by the advertising, encouraged by the taste, animals who eat fruits transport the seeds in their stomachs—and as a parting gesture, conveniently deliver them to their destination complete with a pile of fertilizer.

Autumn's berries nourish everyone from birds to bears. Bright red partridgeberries, growing on a creeping, woody herb that forms evergreen mats in woods, taste dry and seedy to us, but ruffed grouse (a.k.a. partridge), bobwhite quails, wild turkeys, foxes, raccoons, squirrels and mice all love them. Especially in years when acorns and beechnuts are scarce, autumn berries form a staple of the black bear's diet. (One Minnesota study found that in summer, blueberries accounted for one-quarter of everything the bears ate!) Jack-in-the-pulpit offers a stubby club (the remains of "Jack") beaded with bright red or glossy orange berries. Native Americans used to boil and eat the peppery-tasting berries; today the berries mainly nourish thrushes, pheasants and wild turkeys.

Even though toxic to people, poison ivy's white fruit—which shows up brilliantly against its colorful three-part leaves—sustains many species of birds. One naturalist dissected a crow he'd shot and found 153 poison ivy seeds in its stomach. This proves that if you see an animal eat a wild food, this doesn't mean it's safe for you.

Many autumn berries are edible, but consult a field guide before you eat them. (*A Field Guide to Edible Wild Plants* by Lee Allen Peterson also identifies poisonous look-alikes.) Still, you don't have to eat berries to enjoy them. The shrubby juniper's berrylike cones, dark blue with a whitish bloom, provide the infusion that flavors gin. Bayberry's white fruits can be boiled to yield wax for bayberry candles. Dried, spicebush's oval red berries make a substitute for allspice. Like many autumn fruits, spicebush berries stay on the lemony-smelling plant for months—nourishing wildlife, as well as our taste for beauty, all winter long.

Black Bear

The Carnivore in the Rear-View Mirror

A

T FIRST, GRETCHEN VOGEL, who raises ponies, thought it was a horse. Her friend, Dorothy McDonald, who raises labradors, thought it was a dog. But the big black shape the two women saw while they were walking with one of McDonald's dogs in the woods near her home in southern New Hampshire—they realized to their alarm—was a bear.

The dog took off after the bear. McDonald took off after the dog. And Vogel, thinking all the while "that's my friend running after the bear, I really should be helping her," took off as fast as she could—in the opposite direction.

"I've never felt so exposed in my life," said Vogel. "I wanted shelter, a house, a car. I wanted armor."

The bear may have felt the same way. It turned and ran.

None of the parties involved were probably in any danger—except for the dog. Unlike grizzlies and polar bears, the East's black bears almost never attack people (although sows with cubs may make very convincing bluff charges—and black bears west of the Continental Divide, for some reason, are far more aggressive). But this knowledge doesn't diminish the heart-pounding power of an encounter with a wild bear—or the shock of recognition when coming face-to-face with a 200- to 600-pound carnivore who so uncannily reminds us of ourselves.

A generous acorn year, plentiful berries and apples and a promising beechnut crop will keep black bears busy moving and feasting late into fall, likely postponing their search for hibernation dens.

"The longer the food's around, the longer they stay up and party," says Meade Cadot, a biologist who teaches at Antioch/New England Graduate School. Frenzied fall foraging offers the best time of year to spot bears' tracks, claw marks on trees, treetop nesting platforms and distinctive fruit-filled scats. As North America's bear population recovers from three centuries of persecution, your chances of catching a glimpse of the animal itself have never been better.

"Beares they be common, being a great blacke kind of Beare," William Wood wrote of the Boston area in 1634. At that time, more than half a million black bears roamed North America—before bounty hunters and timbermen swarmed the place. Today, with limits on bear hunts and forests recovering, bears are staging a comeback. Experts say 200,000 black bears range the lower 48 states, 40,000 in the East alone. Maine, with more bears than any other eastern state, boasts 19,000.

In some areas, the bears are so thick that they den under porches, wander onto decks, break into garbage cans. One development in Whitingham, Vermont, near the border with Massachusetts, had to call in Vermont's bear research crews and houndsman to run the bears off. (It turned out the developers had poorly bear-proofed their garbage facilities.)

Humans' sloppy habits cause wild bears to lose their normal shyness, stresses James DiStefano, former coordinator of the Vermont Fish and Wildlife Department's bear-rich Southeast District. "They're highly intelligent and learn where to find easy food," he says. Bears are normally active by day. But, explains DiStefano, if they learn a life of garbage-burgling, they become nocturnal, sneaking around homes at night. In Pennsylvania, bear researcher Gary Alt even videotaped a bear who had broken into a home garage and was rummaging through the trunk of a hatchback sedan, looking for something to eat. The bear looked up, spotted its own reflection in the glass of the hatchback window, and—much like a person who's seen a bear—ran away terrified.

One reason bears in human surroundings make such a striking sight is that, in many ways, bears are strangely like us. Bears often stand on their hind legs, and when they do, as when they sit, the front legs hang like arms. Like our hands, their paws are dexterous enough to peel a peach. (The Blackfoot word for the human hand is the same as the word for "bear paw.") Bear tracks, imprints of a heel, arch and toes, "suggest the passing of some large, wild forest person," author David Rockwell observes in his book *Giving Voice to Bear.*

Around the world, throughout human history, people have claimed kinship with bears. The Khanty and Mansi tribes of Siberia say they received fire and weapons from the world's first bear. Many Native American tribes claim a Bear Clan. The ferocious Germanic warriors known as Berserks (*ber*=bear, *serk*=skin), who fought wearing bearskins for armor and were said to be as strong as bears, claimed they could assume ursine form.

Perhaps we have emulated bears in an effort to share their powers, in hopes that we, like bears, could rise from the dead. For bears accomplish this seeming miracle each spring, emerging from the deathly still of hibernation out of gravelike dens in the earth.

In a month or two, when food supplies dwindle and temperatures drop, first the sows, then the yearlings, and finally the boars will seek out individual dens, often under boulders, in rock crevices or in large hollow logs. There, for more than a third of the year, they will neither eat nor drink, neither defecate nor urinate.

Even among the elite club of hibernating animals, bears are unusual. Unlike groundhogs, who can't be roused from their torpor, bears can wake quickly and easily. Sows, for instance, wake to give birth; sometimes bears emerge from a den midwinter, walk around for an hour or so, then go back to sleep for months.

"Bears are metabolic marvels," says Ralph Nelson, an investigator at the University of Illinois. That's why he, along with researchers at the Mayo Clinic and St. Mary's Hospital in San Francisco, is studying the physiology of hibernating black bears, hoping for clues to treating human ailments.

Why don't bears' kidneys overload during hibernation? Why don't their bones weaken, like those of bedridden humans? Noting

BLACK BEARS WILL TAKE ADVANTAGE OF A BOUNTEOUS
CROP OF BEECHNUTS, BERRIES AND APPLES, KEEPING
BUSY AS THEY FEAST AND FORAGE LATE INTO FALL.

that hibernating bears produce energy by burning fat stores but no protein, Nelson is working on developing a low-protein, low-water diet for people with kidney failure, to try to extend the time between hemodialysis treatments. And researchers also suspect that hibernating bears may produce hormones that, if isolated, might yield drugs to protect brittle bones, slow the heartbeat and cool human bodies during surgery.

Prior to denning, black bears put on a layer of fat five inches thick. To this end, black bears are now foraging for acorns, beechnuts, berries, honeycombs, bark, wasp nests, beetles and ants. (Although bears are carnivores, plants make up 80 percent of the black bear's diet. They seldom kill anything bigger than a mouse.) If a bear's been grocery shopping in your area, you can tell: they overturn large rocks, tear apart bees' nests, scrape bark off trees, break off the limbs of fruit trees and rip open rotted logs. You'll see the menu plainly in bear scat. Within the distinctive, cylindrical mass, this time of year you'll usually find lots of apple and berry seeds.

Look overhead for more bear sign. In the crowns of oaks and beech, bears often pull the tips of the branches inward, simultaneously reaching the nuts at the twig ends and constructing a springy treetop sleeping platform. It looks like a six-times life-size eagle nest.

Down the trunk, you might find claw marks. Bears sometimes claw and rub favorite trees, even if they don't climb them. Five-pointed pinpricks mean a bear visited very recently; if you are especially lucky, you might also find fur and smell a wild, sour scent. As the clawed bark scars over, the marks enlarge with time.

Listen as well as look. Bears don't often vocalize, but when they do, they can sound uncannily like people.

A few autumns back, up near the woods where he lives in Chesuncook, Maine, Bert McBurnie heard what he thought was a man behind him calling. He called back: "Hey-y-y!" McBurnie turned around and spotted a figure a few hundred feet away: "Merciful Jesus!" he thought. "It's a BEAR!" That ended the conversation on McBurnie's part.

The bear, perhaps perplexed by the sudden silence, then sniffed the ground where McBurnie had earlier trod. At the scent, the bear realized its mistake. It stood, let out a wail—which McBurnie translates roughly as "Merciful Jesus! It's a PERSON!"—then turned and ran back into the woods.

Hand-Feeding Wild Birds

A Bird in Hand . . . Is Worth the Wait

H UGH WIBERG often walked through Topsfield Wildlife Sanctuary in Massachusetts to savor the peace and the exercise. One chilly morning, as he rounded a bend on the path, about 50 feet ahead of him he saw a man standing alone, stock-still, his left hand extended. Unseen, Wiberg stopped to watch.

Less than a minute later, a chickadee darted from the bush and landed on the man's hand. Soon, a black and white flurry of tiny birds surrounded the lone figure. Chickadee after chickadee fluttered to the outstretched hand to land, grab a seed and fly off.

Wiberg stood there watching for 10 minutes, amazed. Curious though he was, when he finally left the scene, Wiberg departed silently, without introducing himself or asking questions. He couldn't bear to break the spell it seemed the stranger had woven with the birds.

That was 20 years ago. Wiberg, who manages Mahoney's Rocky Ledge Nursery in Winchester, Massachusetts, still visits Topsfield—but these days he always brings pocketfuls of filberts, pecans, walnuts, Brazil nuts and sunflower seeds. Within minutes of his arrival at his regular spots, the birds fly in to meet him: not only black-capped chickadees, but also titmice, nuthatches and others. There's one particular male cardinal he's known for three years who eats out of his hand but won't land on it. "One of my goals," he says, "is to get that male cardinal standing on my hand."

Ever since folks began coaxing wild birds to backyard feeding stations well over a century ago, people have been trying to draw the birds ever closer. *Wild Bird Guests*, a book which began as a series of articles published in *The Boston Transcript* in 1904, was perhaps the first to detail how to entice wild birds to take seed from the hand; ever since, people have been coming up with improvements and variations.

Alfred Martin, the Maine birder who wrote *Hand Taming Wild Birds at the Feeder* in 1967, suggested you talk to the birds you are feeding. Len Howard, the British bird behaviorist, insists you should stay so still you try not to even swallow. John Dyett, who lives in Greenfield, New Hampshire, trained birds to trust him by using a scarecrow; he set seed out on a dummy dressed up in old clothes and a hat, and after the birds learned to eat from it, he took the clothes off the dummy and changed into them himself.

In his book *Hand-Feeding Wild Birds*, Wiberg suggests none of these gimmicks, focusing instead on patience and offering the foods the birds love to eat. Among his findings are that birds prefer crumbled nutmeats to sunflower seeds but like sunflower seeds much better than mixed birdseed; blue jays and nuthatches love Cheez-Its.

But on one point, all agree: birds won't learn overnight to trust you enough to land on your hand. "Think of hand-feeding birds as a process, not an event," Wiberg advises in his book. Building trust takes some time. Now is the best time to start, while it's cold enough for the birds to welcome the treats, and early enough that winter still stretches before you. If you start in November, by February you can have birds flocking to your hand.

You can start at your backyard feeder or, if you prefer, start setting out seed at a quiet clearing in the woods of your local reserve or park. The birds will quickly learn its location and visit it regularly. Go out in the morning, between 7:00 and 9:30, and stand or sit, quiet and motionless, about 15 feet away from the feeding site. After 20 or 30 minutes, slowly back away and go inside.

Wiberg spent only half an hour on Saturdays and Sundays with his birds early on. Each Saturday, he would close the gap between himself and the feeder by a foot or two. After eight weeks, he waited with his seed-filled hand right on the feeder. By the eleventh weekend, his hand replaced the feeder.

Black-capped chickadees are, beyond doubt, the boldest birds you'll encounter. They're usually the first to appear at the backyard feeder, and they'll be the first to come to seed you set out regularly at a park. Maine birder Alfred Martin found some far northern birds, like the grey jay, common redpoll, pine grosbeak and evening grosbeak, relatively quick to brave the unknown territory of the human hand. Titmice, who often travel in company with chickadees, may learn from their bolder companions, after many visits, to feed from a human hand. Harder to entice are cardinals, woodpeckers and sparrows. At the shore, seagulls eagerly eat from the hand, and in the South, so will pelicans.

"Devoid of their inherent fear of man, birds are much more likely to reveal their true selves" when they alight on the hand, Nantucket birder and author John Dennis claims. Often, at close range, birds reveal themselves as individuals. Each November, Wiberg looks for the previous season's special friends—like Black Bart, the white-breasted nuthatch he's been meeting each year since 1988. He always recognized Tom Titmouse—the first titmouse Wiberg ever fed, who continued to fly to his hand for three years—by his personality. "He came zapping down to me with no hesitation, his crest right up." (Like many crested birds, titmice fold theirs when they feel nervous.) For five years, a one-footed chickadee Wiberg called Peg Leg used to accompany him in Topsfield, often riding on his shoulder. Wiberg last saw Peg Leg in March of 1990. "I still miss him," Wiberg confesses.

Does hand-feeding threaten the birds in any way? No less an authority than Roger Tory Peterson—who has fed many a chickadee from his hands—says no. Most bird experts agree hand-feeding is no more intrusive than erecting a bird feeder—which 65 million Americans are doing already, at last count. Fears that birds become dependent on these hand-outs were somewhat calmed by a recent

University of Wisconsin Department of Wildlife Ecology study. Two groups of chickadees—one feeder-fed, the other sans supplements—were monitored over three years before the feeder-fed birds went cold turkey. Survival rates for the two groups were then compared over several years. There was no difference.

What's the difference between feeding birds from a close-by feeder and feeding them direct from the hand? "It puts me, personally, into direct, immediate contact with a wild creature," says Wiberg—a joy he began sharing with his granddaughter, who fed a chickadee from her hand when she was only two. "It's a strange and mystical feeling when, 12 inches from my eyes, a black-capped chickadee is looking back at me," says the grandfather, "and it doesn't lessen with the passage of time."

For a Plant, It's a Galling Experience

꩜

YOU'LL PROBABLY FIRST NOTICE the silhouettes. Naked against the sky, the branches of a certain tree may look bumpy, as if drawn with a leaky pen. Or a bush whose leaves and fruits dropped long ago still seems festooned, as if hung with Christmas ornaments.

For many plants, summer's leaves, like clothing, covered a multitude of imperfections, now laid bare. "At close range, nature is deformed," naturalists Ed Duensing and A.B. Millmoss observe in their nature guidebook, *The Backyard and Beyond.* If you look closer at these bumps and lumps, you'll see what they mean: you'll find cylindrical swellings covered with red hair, succulent-looking orbs hanging like fruit, seedlike bumps on leaves, oozing tumorous masses.

Certain trees may even take on alter egos. Willows seem to sprout pinecones. Oaks may seem laden with apples. Of course, oaks don't have apples. Willows don't have pinecones. But they may have galls.

Galls are created by invaders who chemically co-opt their host plants into growing these deformities in place of a normal bud, branch, flower, leaf or root. If you cut open the gall, you might see the culprit behind the mischief: usually it's the pale, legless, innocent-looking larva of a tiny fly or a stingless wasp.

From the plant's point of view, a gall is a defensive barrier. Most galls don't hurt the plant, and usually fall off after a year or so. But from the point of view of the invader, the gall offers both food and shelter in luxuriant abundance.

Galls may occur on well over 2,000 different species of plants; oaks seem particularly prone. Some appear on stems, some on bark, others on leaves, some on flowers, even roots. Although galls are "abnormal" structures, they are surprisingly common and often alarmingly numerous. Some plants are so beset with galls that the weight of the structures can bow their branches. One large oak outside Albany, New York, covered with the giant, beadlike swellings of the gouty oak gall, was estimated to host some 500,000 baby wasps in its galls.

Michael Quinn, a Vermont teacher, photographer and gall enthusiast, almost lost a friend in an argument over the pineapple-shaped structures she spotted on the branches of a particular willow. "She simply wouldn't believe it could be a gall—she insisted that something that abundant had to be a fruit," he said. In the spring, at the Garden in the Woods in Framingham, Massachusetts, it takes three people several days to pluck all the bright green, golfball-sized galls off the azaleas. (These look like juicy fruits, and in fact, the Appalachian Cherokee used to harvest them as sweet-sour treats.)

Garden staff pluck galls for cosmetic reasons. Some people find them unsettling. Even the word sounds like bad news: Biblical authors used "wormwood and gall" to evoke the bitterness and sorrow of the destruction of Jerusalem. At the Arnold Arboretum in Boston, Director of Living Collections Peter Del Tredici prefers to call galls "swellings," and when they're on wood, "burls." Burls are nice—woodworkers love them. Burls on black cherry, sugar maple, redwood and black walnut are highly prized; sawn and polished, a burl yields beautiful swirling, figured patterns in the wood. But call the same structure a gall, Del Tredici says, and plant pathologists "become terribly excited and upset."

Some galls—the 5 percent or so caused by viruses, bacteria or fungi—can kill the plant. Fissured, tumorlike galls on olive trees impart a rancid, bitter taste to the fruit. The presence of these olive galls is among the oldest of recorded plant diseases; Socrates' successor, Theophrastus, complained about them 2,000 years ago. (Scientists now know these galls are caused by a bacterium.) Crown gall, one of the most-studied plant diseases, afflicts fruit, nut and ornamental trees and is also caused by a bacterium.

But most galls are caused by insects, representing a fascinating, ancient evolutionary link between plant and animal. Millions of years ago, the progenitors of today's gall-making insects probably just munched on their host plants, and that was that. But over time, certain flies, wasps, mites and wormlike, soil-dwelling nematodes evolved chemicals to mimic their host plants' own growth hormones. Once these chemicals are released—by the action of the larva feeding, or sometimes by the egg in which the larva is encased—the plant responds in two major ways. Cells proliferate abnormally around the site, and the plant shunts extra sugars there.

When Jorie Hunken, a naturalist in Woodstock, Connecticut, tells children about galls, she asks the kids to imagine they're each a baby gall wasp: "When you're hungry, all you do is roll over and take a bite of your bed—a sweet, gooey, spongy, edible mattress."

Some galls ooze with sugars. In his 1918 book *Key to American Insect Galls*, Ephriam Porter Felt, former New York State Entomologist (and virtual dean of American galls), recorded a large pin oak near Newton, New Jersey, which people called "the roaring tree" because it seemed to hum or roar. The sound was coming from the hosts of bees and flies attracted by the sweet fluids oozing from its numerous galls.

Some galls also yield commercially valuable dyes. Certain oak galls contain a high-quality pigment, a tannin, that the U.S. Treasury and the Bank of England use in preparing the inks to print currency.

Cut open a gall and you might find its architect inside. (Remember, this won't hurt the plant, but damaging the gall dooms any inhabitant.) The pale, legless larva of a gnatlike fly overwinters in the willow cone gall, emerging in early spring as an adult. A ball-shaped swelling on the dried stem of goldenrod shelters the larva of a different fly. But you might find a beetle larva in there instead—this species parasitizes the fly larva, and then takes over the nursery as its own.

Some galls this time of year are empty. If you slice open an oak apple gall in the summer, you'll find a seedlike capsule inside, where the young of a stingless wasp is maturing. By fall, the gall has dried to a mass of fibers radiating from the center of the capsule to the now-papery skin, and the wasp has hatched and flown. Likewise, elliptical galls on goldenrods are now empty. Look near the top of the gall for the exit hole. Here an adult moth emerged from its reddish brown pupal case in September, chewing its way out.

But an exit hole doesn't necessarily mean no one's home. Often after the original occupants have left, spiders and mites move in, glad for the winter shelter.

Cougars Stage a Comeback

≈

AS THEY STOOD LOOKING OUT OVER A RISE one crisp autumn day in 1987, Leandre Poisson and Howard Mansfield spotted a very large, low-slung, tawny-colored animal walking leisurely across a pasture on Poisson's property in Harrisville, New Hampshire.

It was so big and moved so distinctively that the two men knew immediately what it was. Poisson dashed inside to get binoculars. The two shared the field glasses as they watched the creature for the next 10 minutes. It had the head and body of a maneless lion, and a long, thick tail.

No other native cat has a tail like this. The men knew they were watching a mountain lion, a cougar, a puma, an eastern panther— the largest predator ever to roam the northeastern United States.

What they didn't realize was this: there weren't supposed to be any mountain lions left in the northeastern U.S. Yet many times before and after the animal appeared in Poisson's field, people have reported seeing mountain lions where there weren't supposed to be any. In Massachusetts, well over 200 sightings have been filed with fish and game officials in the last 10 years. Cougars have been seen in New Jersey. Folks in Pennsylvania say they've found cougar kills— deer carcasses covered with sticks and debris.

But no one has taken the photograph, filmed the video, found the carcass or cast the track that proves to everyone's satisfaction that wild mountain lions are indeed back, living in the most densely populated portion of the United States.

41

Only one instance of these numerous sightings has been accepted by wildlife officials as the real thing: Mark Walker, a Massachusetts resident visiting his mother, saw three mountain lions strolling through the woods together in Vermont's Green Mountains on April 2, 1994—and his sighting was confirmed by the discovery of mountain lion droppings. The scat was analyzed by the U.S. Fish and Wildlife Service's forensic lab in Oregon; it contained hairs the animal had swallowed after grooming itself, which allowed a positive identification. The Vermont Fish and Wildlife Department issued a press release citing "hard evidence of cougars in the wild in Vermont."

But what about these other sightings elsewhere in the East?

How could such a large predator go undetected by wildlife workers for so long? Even out West, where cougar numbers have risen steadily over the past decade, the cats are elusive. There are an estimated 5,000 cougars in California, 2,000 in Idaho, 2,500 in British Columbia and perhaps 700 in Alberta. Susan C. Morse, a forester and wildlife habitat consultant based in Jericho, Vermont, has been visiting lion country in these areas for the past 10 years as part of what she calls a "personal quest" to learn more about the animal and its living requirements. It was two years before she saw her first cougar.

Unlike bobcats, cougars are not usually aggressive. Still, the western comeback of such an impressive predator has spawned some controversy and concern. Two joggers have been killed in the past five years by cougars, one in California and one in Colorado. A human running by in front of a young, inexperienced cougar is almost as irresistible as a string wiggling on the floor in front of a kitten. In the state of Washington, a cyclist glanced over his shoulder to see a cougar loping alongside him on a fire road. But once the cyclist wisely halted the bike, the cat lost interest. Cougar experts believe these were all young mountain lions testing new, marginal habitats—since people have left cougars so little room. Howard Quigley, president of the Hornocker Wildlife Research Institute in Moscow, Idaho, notes that dangerous incidents involving lions and humans are rare. During the past 100 years, there have been fewer than 60 documented attacks by cougars on people. Even though these days people are seeing more lions, Quigley points out that "mountain lions are able to watch humans a great deal more easily than we can observe them." So far, they have mostly watched us harmlessly.

Cougars are conservative creatures. In Alberta, Morse tracked one female who ate from the carcass of a single moose calf for 13 days. And mountain lions usually shrink from people. In Orange County, California, Morse tracked a tom cougar who used a culvert under an eight-lane highway to get to and from one part of his territory without being seen. Yet, in the East, where Morse has been "tracking all sorts of critters" for more than two decades, she has yet to see even one footprint of a mountain lion. "That doesn't prove they're not here," she says. "It only means they're not where we're looking for them."

The quest to find wild cougars in the Northeast has been, in the words of one writer, like chasing a ghost.

Tom French, assistant director for Natural Heritage and Endangered Species programs at the Massachusetts Division of Fisheries and Wildlife, has had plenty of experience with reports of sightings of unusual creatures. "The mountain lion is definitely the most interesting of the phantoms of the woods that people call in about," he says.

But unlike other phantoms, the mountain lion is a known species, a creature who used to exist in the Northeast, and who, indeed, belongs right where folks are saying it is.

The mountain lion was once one of the most widespread large mammals in the New World, found from Alaska to South America. In Colonial times, they were so numerous that many areas offered bounties for them. Even zoologists and conservationists urged on the eradication effort: in 1913, the director of the New York Zoological Society told forestry students at Yale that "the eradication of the puma . . . is a task of immediate urgency."

Like so many native mammals, the catamount—as many New

England locals once called it—was extinguished by the turn of the century.

Or so people thought. Where, otherwise, could the phantom cougars be coming from?

Undoubtedly, some of the well-meaning folks who reported cougar sightings really saw something else. But most wildlife officials agree that not all these reports are cases of mistaken identity. "I'm not skeptical that lions are here," says Morse. "I'm skeptical that an indigenous wild population is here generally, throughout, for instance, New England."

Some of the mountain lions people report seeing could be escaped pets. Strange as it sounds, people do keep them. And as long as they have a permit, it's legal. In Massachusetts alone, more than 50 people have such permits.

But could escaped pets account for all the evidence? Friends of the Eastern Panther, an alliance of lion fans based in Exeter, New Hampshire, thinks not. The nearest acknowledged populations of mountain lions are in Florida, where an extensive effort is under way to bring the species back from the brink of extinction. Then there's the population in Montana, and further west. But, Friends maintains, there could be another unacknowledged population as near as New Brunswick in eastern Canada. These forested lands, the alliance believes, could be the "refuge" from which the migrants set out.

A few springs back, Friends of the Eastern Panther mounted a search for signs of mountain lion along the Fundy Bay region of the province. Morse was on that team, along with two biologists and several volunteers. On snowshoes, on snowmobiles, in airplanes, they scoured the land for cougar prints, cougar scat, cougar kills. They found nothing.

But that doesn't prove the animals are not there. Or in the northeastern U.S.

Elizabeth Marshall Thomas, author of *The Tribe of Tiger: Cats and Their Culture*, has tracked mountain lions in Idaho, held wild mountain lion cubs in her arms and spent time at close range with a tame mountain lion named Ruby (so close that the adult lioness sucked peacefully on Thomas's arm). So Thomas knows what she saw, one recent winter, when she looked out the window of her home in southern New England: a tawny cat, bigger than a bobcat, with a tail thick as a child's arm. And she believes there are plenty more where that one came from.

"Why shouldn't there be mountain lions?" she asks. "There were no coyotes here 30 years ago—a western animal no one had ever heard of. But they're here now. Why not mountain lions?"

If the mountain lion—like the eagle and the fisher, the bear and bobcat—is making a return to the Northeast, this is important news. As Donald Schueler writes in his book *Incident at Eagle Ranch*, "The mountain lion works a strong magic in the imagination of many Americans. It is the ultimate loner, a renegade presence in the wildest canyons and wildest mountains, the sign of everything that is remote from us, everything we have not spoiled."

If the Northeast's top predator is back, it's a sign that the land is recovering from the abuses of 100 years ago—and a sign of a brief, vital opportunity to protect the wild lands that remain in this crowded, "civilized" corner of the world. "It's like we have a second chance," says Morse. "If mountain lions are here, it's because they deserve to be here."

Winter

Sounds and Silences
of December

ECEMBER IS THE GRAY MONTH. The sky is gray. Lakes and ponds are gray. The bark of trees looks gray. The few, dead leaves that still cling to the gray branches have weathered from brown and yellow to gray. Before it is blanketed with brilliant white snow, even the ground looks gray.

Not only the colors have gone gray, but also, it seems, the fruits of most other senses. December's cold numbs the skin, the tongue, the nostrils. The frozen ground locks up the scent of the earth.

But as if to make up for the void of colors muted, touch numbed, scents sealed, December's sounds are the year's most vibrant. Hearing may be the richest sense: Helen Keller wrote she felt its absence a handicap far more severe than blindness. This month, hearing packs a bigger wallop than at any other time.

"Winter is the best time of year for sounds," asserts Eric Orff, New Hampshire's Region III wildlife biologist. At no other time of year are sounds so sharp: the early drumming of the pileated woodpecker. The booming of ice on a lake. Wind whispering through pines or howling through oaks. Trees creaking eerily, like rusty hinges. The scolding "dee-dee-dee!" of the chickadee. "Their call in the cold air reaches out and grabs you like Ma Bell," says Orff.

There are physical reasons why December's sounds seem to ring so clear. Bill Barklow, a Framingham (Massachusetts) College biologist and an expert on acoustics, explains that sounds travel farther over frozen ground. When the ground is frozen, usually the atmosphere above is warmer, which makes the sound bounce back to-

ward the ground. December's freeze "is like having a sound reflec-
tor in the sky," he says. The effect is the same as a voice carried far
over the cool water of a lake in summer.

December's bareness amplifies and clarifies its voices. Later in
the winter, deep snow will suck up sound, absorbing vibrations.
Spring and summer are crowded with ambient noise: the songs of
birds and insects, the whisper of grasses and leaves, the rustle of small
animals in the woods, not to mention cars and people and dogs
enjoying the seasons of warmth—it's difficult to pick out any one
sound. During the leafy months, foliage absorbs and reflects much
sound—especially the higher frequencies. (This, Barklow explains,
is why low-frequency sounds, such as the infrasonic calls of whales,
hippos and elephants, travel so far: these gently rolling waves of
sound can go around objects in their path, unlike the higher frequencies that humans hear.)

But when the ground is hard and trees bare and summertime's
murmuring hushed, sound slices through the air—stark, clear, pure.

Sounds not only carry far, but seem crisper. Frozen surfaces are
rock-hard and don't absorb any of the sound; instead, sound is
reflected.

This is the time of year Orff likes to hike up a mountain at night,
just to sit and savor the sounds. Nights are best for listening, he
maintains; there's less car noise from neighboring highways, since
fewer folks are on the road. "On clear, starry nights, the sounds are
sharp, sharp, sharp!" he says.

One of winter's loudest voices belongs to ice, booming and
cracking as it expands and contracts. Many of us are scared by the
sound—particularly if we're skating on it—but to some nature
lovers, nothing could be more melodious: "To me, it's like a song,"
says New Hampshire naturalist and wilderness guide John Kulish.
The bigger the pond, the louder the sound.

Trees also boom. One moonlit winter night, Orff remembers,
"the trees, the hardwoods and beech, they were popping like fire-
works." These loud popping sounds aren't what you might suspect.
They're not caused by the wind cracking branches off—that's a dif-

ferent sound. Nor is this due to the trees' sap freezing and bursting, like a bottle of juice bursts in the freezer. Hardwoods shunt most of their liquids down to their roots, below the frost line, explains Antioch/New England Graduate School ecologist Tom Wessels; conifers' sap doesn't form ice crystals.

It's easier to tell what doesn't cause the popping than what does. The sound mystifies even botanists and foresters. "We've all heard it," says forester William Guenther of Windham County, Vermont, "but none of us seem to know exactly what causes it."

Wessels offers this guess: the wood of trees, particularly hardwoods, expands and contracts during dramatic changes in temperature. (This, adds Wessels, is why the only broadleaf trees found from latitudes above northern Quebec are light-barked birches and aspens. At these latitudes, winter's low-slanting sun would heat up dark bark so much, and then darkness cool it so fast, the trees would literally crack up.)

If you go out on a sound safari this winter, remember to stay quiet yourself. This means staying still, so make sure you're dressed far more warmly than you'd need to be for a hike. You don't have to be *in* the wind to hear it: choose a sheltered location to sit—you'll stay warmer, so you can listen longer. If you want company, choose a companion who'll heed Epictetus the Stoic's 2,000-year-old advice: "God gave man two ears but one mouth that he might hear twice as much as he speaks."

To better pick up faraway sounds, assume what Casanovia, New York, naturalist and author Ed Duensing calls the "Big Ear Position": cup your hands behind your ears and push the outer ear forward with thumb and index finger. "This movement will make whatever you are listening to sound louder, almost as if someone had turned up the volume," he advises. (In fact, to see how well it works, try this trick at home: Turn the volume down on the TV until you can hear the sound, but not the words, from across the room. Then try the Big Ear Position. The words, Duensing promises, will come in loud and clear.)

But remember that one of the greatest rewards of listening can

be silence. Orchestras know this: at the end of a performance of
Mozart's Fantasy in C Minor, for example, you can hear a pin drop
as a thousand ears strain for the last note. December's silence—quite
different from, say, the soft, glowing stillness of a rare, windless night
in early March—is almost piercing—clear, cleansing. Savor the
silences as well as the sounds of December.

Flying Squirrels

Furry Frisbees

෫෧

PIECE TOGETHER THESE CLUES: squirrels' tracks in the snow come out of nowhere. A flattened grayish, feathery, four-inch tail lies severed in the driveway. At night, tiny toe-nails click against your bird feeder.

These tell-tale signs are tip-offs to a fact you might never suspect: that at night, when red and gray squirrels are snug in their tree holes, tiny, feather-light flying squirrels are gliding through the dark like furry Frisbees.

North America's two species of flying squirrels don't actually fly; they glide. The northern flying squirrel frequents spruce and fir forests from New England to Canada and over much of the northern United States. The southern flying squirrel prefers hardwood forests along most of the East Coast. The two species look virtually alike, although the southern is slightly smaller. The little creature's two-ounce body seems to be wrapped up in a cinnamon-gray coat several sizes too big. At rest, all this loose skin folds up beneath the rodent's soft white belly like an accordion. But when the squirrel leaps from a height, the furry membranes stretch to form a combination of parachute and kite, enabling the animal to glide distances of more than 100 feet.

And flying squirrels are more common than people think. One study estimated that in wooded areas, they may be as numerous as two or three per acre. In the winter, they're easier to spot because hunger may drive them to backyard bird feeders, and cold compels them to huddle in tree holes, attics and outbuildings in groups of up to 20.

FLYING SQUIRRELS ARE MORE COMMON THAN
PEOPLE REALIZE, BUT BECAUSE THEY ARE ACTIVE ONLY
AFTER DARK, IT IS EASY TO BE UNAWARE OF THEM.

One biologist calls flying squirrels "the ultimate babyschema"—which means that people instinctively find them, like human babies, almost irresistibly adorable. They're smaller than chipmunks and covered with incredibly soft fur. They stare up at you with enormous black eyes "so big and dark and beautiful," says 16-year-old Virginia Cadot, who has helped raise orphaned baby squirrels, "they look like they see everything."

(Well, not everything. The severed tail you found in the driveway came from a flying squirrel—the only part the cat or owl spat out.)

Because flying squirrels are active only after dark, most people never even guess these little mammals are there. But if by day you spot signs of flying squirrels in your area, all you may have to do is stock the bird feeder with sunflower seeds, turn on the back porch light and watch the nightly show.

That's what Ernest and Nancy Adams do each winter. One night they heard a funny noise at the kitchen window, where they had hung their bird feeder. So Nancy turned on the outside light, looked out the window "and there, two inches from our faces, was a flying squirrel, looking at us with bright, beady eyes."

It turned out there were at least four of them, each taking its turn gliding out of a tree, swooping to the feeder. All winter, the family watched the acrobatics. After climbing to what it deemed an appropriate height, each squirrel would first bob to the left, then to the right, calculating its flight. Then, having triangulated the path, it would launch itself from the tree, throwing its arms forward and out and its legs backward and out, unfurling the flying membrane like Superman's cape. By raising and lowering its arms, the flying squirrel steers; the tail acts as stabilizer. As it approaches a landing, the airborne rodent lowers its tail and hind feet and embraces its target hind feet first. If it lands on a tree, it immediately runs around the other side of the trunk, to foil any predators who might have watched the flight.

"It is incredible how rapidly they climb and how sure-footed they are," observes Ernest P. Walker, who, as former director of the

National Zoo, is certainly a connoisseur of animal athletes. He's seen
North American flying squirrels glide for 165 feet and has clocked
them at a leisurely rate of just over 4 miles per hour. (Several species
of Asia's giant flying squirrels, who grow up to two feet long and
weigh as much as six pounds, can glide up to 1,500 feet, sometimes
riding ascending currents of air coming up deep valleys.)

Of course, not everyone has flying squirrels outside their windows. Some people have them right inside the house.

Before their daughter, Virginia, was born, Cynthia and Meade
Cadot, administrators at the Harris Center for Conservation Education in Hancock, New Hampshire, raised an orphaned flying
squirrel they named Amelia. She used to sleep in the pockets of coats
hanging in the closet. "When we had company, we had to frisk
everyone on the way out to make sure they didn't have our flying
squirrel in their coat pocket," Meade says. (In case you're considering making a flying squirrel a pet, think again: "From a housekeep-
ing point of view, a flying squirrel is not ideal," says Meade
delicately. Most tree-dwelling animals are careless about their toilet, since gravity makes everything below them a potential latrine.)

And flying squirrels are dangerously smart. More flying squirrels became the Cadots' wards seven years ago after a neighborhood
cat ate their mother. The growing orphans soon learned how to
unlatch the cage door and frisk about the house at night—though in
the morning, they'd all be back snug in their cage as if nothing had
happened. (The jig was up when, one morning, Virginia discovered one of the squirrels asleep behind a book in the bookcase.)

Flying squirrels can get into your house even if you don't invite
them. During the winter, they forsake their summer nests (often
refurbished woodpecker holes) for larger quarters, where up to 20
sleeping squirrels may huddle for warmth. Not uncommonly, they
nest in attics, and from there may find their way further inside. (Occasionally, someone finds a flying squirrel mysteriously drowned in
the toilet.)

Lee Elmer, a retiree in her 70s, thought she lived alone in her
Great Neck, Long Island, home—until she saw a head peering at her

from the top of the flowered orange curtains of her living room. "Look!" she cried out to a visiting friend—and at that moment, the creature glided across the living room.

The intruder lived inside the house for two weeks, pilfering cream-filled wafers and careening across the rooms. Peanut butter bait finally enticed it into a live-trap three nights before New Year's Day. Elmer called a wildlife organization to come take the animal away.

As relieved as Elmer was to be rid of her flying squirrel, the Adamses were missing theirs. One winter, their flying squirrels failed to reappear. Ernest may have discovered the reason why earlier when, one night in the fall, he flicked on the outside kitchen light and noticed an owl sitting on the feeder.

Pines

The Trees that Soften Winter's Winds

ON A COLD, BLUSTERY NIGHT, listen to the winter wind. It howls through the naked branches of oaks, snaps limbs off maples, rips branches from beeches and birches. Yet the wind always speaks softly to the pines. Listen: when it has reached the plumelike boughs of a pine tree, the north wind merely sighs.

A botanist will tell you that this is because of the structure of the tree's leaves. All conifers—hemlocks, spruces, cedars, pines and firs—are specially designed to withstand winter snows and winds. They do not need to lose all their leaves in autumn; they drop them throughout the year. Because these leaves are stiff and slender, conifers' needles shed snow, and the wind slips harmlessly through them. The pines' needles, held in distinctive bundles of two to five leaves, are the longest and softest of them all. The needles literally soften the wind's blows.

That's the botanist's story. But a Greek myth offers a different explanation for the sound of the winter wind through the pines.

The ancients told that Boreas, the north wind, loved a nymph named Pitys. Her beauty also attracted the attention of Pan, the piper. Jealous Boreas couldn't stand the idea that Pan might steal away his beloved. So that no other could have her, Boreas blew Pitys over a cliff, to cast her into the sea. But compassionate gods intervened. They changed the nymph, as she was falling off the rocky cliff, into the first pine tree.

This, the myth tells us, is why pines grow in rocky and sandy soil; and this is why the north wind whispers in the pines: wind and pine are lovers still.

For, like all the needle-leaved evergreens, pines send pollen from one blossom to another on the wind. The long yellow streaks you see on ponds near evergreen woods are pine pollen.

Since at least the time of the Pagans, who first thought of bringing evergreen trees indoors to celebrate winter festivals, conifers have softened the psychological blows of winter. Though few people choose pines as Christmas trees—the blue-green, spire-shaped balsam fir is the most popular—of all the winter-cheering evergreens, pines are arguably the most inspiring.

A pine appeared on the Massachusetts Colonial shilling and was later incorporated into the state's coat of arms. The first flag of the American Revolutionary forces bore a white pine. Maine, the Pine Tree State, once had the tree on its license plates (now, a lobster).

If America's early settlers were looking for just another pretty evergreen to symbolize their pride, they could have chosen the symmetrical fir. But as naturalist Maud Going has pointed out, "Pines attain symmetry only when they live in peace and plenty. It seems more probable," she wrote in her 1903 book *With the Trees*, "that in the pine, living on hard fare and smitten by ocean gales, yet undaunted and ever green, they saw a type of their struggling commonwealth and a happy augury for its future."

In fact, the earliest settlers' first riches were pines. Most treasured was the five-needled white pine. "Perhaps no other tree in the world has had so momentous a career," writes Donald Culross Peattie in *A Natural History of Trees of East and Central North America*. "Certainly no other has played so great a role in the life and history of the American people."

Settlers were astonished by vast stands of white pines all over New England, towering 150 feet and taller; on the current site of Dartmouth College, a tree 240 feet tall was cut. Pioneers said a squirrel could travel a lifetime without coming down out of a white pine. Soaring straight and thick for 80 feet without a first branch, its soft, strong, light, elastic wood was perfectly suited to ship masts.

Before long, Colonists were exporting white pine to Portugal, Spain and Africa—though England's monarchy reserved the tallest specimens for its Royal Navy. These trees were marked with a three-stripe blaze known as the King's Broad Arrow. It is said that some of these 175-foot trees, known as the Carlisle Pines, are still standing in Carlisle, Massachusetts, though the blaze has long faded.

If true, they miraculously escaped the ax. By 1890, according to most historical accounts, the only virgin white pine left was in the southern Appalachian mountains.

Yet pines are still economically important. The more durable, though brittler, wood of the Norway pine (though it sounds like a foreign species, it was so named because the first specimen sent to Kew Gardens came from Norway, Maine) provides most of eastern North America's telephone poles, log cabins and dock pilings. Along U.S. highways, you often see big, same-age stands of Norway pine, with their distinctive red, armorlike plates of bark. These trees were planted in the 1930s by the Civilian Conservation Corps.

Though the ancient giants are gone, white pine is still important for building furniture and for siding. So important in some areas, in fact, that you can't get a gooseberry pie in Vermont. The gooseberry shrub can host destructive white pine blister rust, and for that reason, most of the wild gooseberries were destroyed in that state in the 1950s. It's now illegal even to ship gooseberry bushes to Vermont.

The pines offer more subtle joys standing than cut. In winter, the snow of pine forests records many tracks. Red squirrels and nuthatches love the cone-borne seeds. Deer browse the lower branches; rabbits nibble the young leaves.

People can eat the tree, too: in May and June, the inner bark of white pine is good to chew. Early New Englanders candied strips of it. (The pine nuts used in pesto are from a European species, the stone pine.)

And though firs and spruce bear cones as well, pinecones are the favorites for Christmas ornaments. In the Pine Barrens of New Jersey, "pine ballers" pick about 3,000 cones a day from dwarf pitch pines for the Christmas business.

But perhaps the pines are most lovely for the music they provide on blustery winter nights. Today, in the voice of the north wind as it blows through the long, soft needles of pine, we can imagine the conversation of Boreas and Pitys. Or is it the flute of the piper, Pan?

When Deer Last in the Dooryard Browsed

LATE ONE DECEMBER AFTERNOON, Cynthia Cadot looked out the window of her office, in an old estate in the tiny town of Hancock, New Hampshire, to find an odd sight: three deer walking up the stairs.

The deer, two fawns and their mother, mounted the big stone steps leading from a field to the grassy terrace, and paused to nibble at the evergreens forming an ornamental archway over a second set of steps. Then they climbed these steps, too, their half-moon hooves clicking like high heels on the granite. Finally, they walked on across the lawn to eat the foundation plantings.

They stayed an hour, while Cadot watched, rapt. "We haven't seen deer come that close since we first came up here in 1975," she said. But there they were the next day, again.

This is usually the time of year that deer move away from areas where people live. Now's the time they normally seek out their traditional "deer yards"—typically among stands of dense evergreens, especially hemlock, beneath whose needled canopies snow is shallower and easier to navigate.

But every once in a while comes a year when deer aren't in their yards, but in yours.

True, each year, it seems, there are more and more deer. Come winter, there are reports of white-tailed deer eating bushes around suburban homes, crowding airport runways, harassing orchardists by nibbling new buds off the apple trees. Bucks even sometimes use garden fences to help dislodge wobbly antlers, which they shed, one at a time, each winter. (If you're lucky, you might find one before mineral-hungry mice nibble them away.) Deer numbers are on the increase, because —among other reasons—humans have so altered the landscape: We've killed off most deer predators and carved lawns out of the forest, creating edges deer love to frequent. Then we plant their favorite foods by the foundations of our homes.

But lots of deer doesn't necessarily translate to the sort of spectacular views Cadot enjoyed. Where you're most likely to find them depends upon many factors. Whitetails' activities reflect the influence of autumn acorns and winter snows—as well as the herd's own traditions and knowledge.

Consider the acorn crop—which deer in many areas depend upon heavily for food. After several good years, often the local crop fails entirely. Red oak takes two years to grow a ripe acorn; any of the spring frosts or winter storms over the preceding two years could do it in. (And if this happens, you'll see more gray squirrels and flying squirrels at your bird feeder.)

Winter snow—or lack of it—also figures in the picture. "For the deer, winter officially begins as soon as 15 inches of snow has accumulated," says William Porter, a deer biologist at State University of New York's College of Environmental Science and Forestry in Syracuse. That's when the snow gets so deep that the deer can lift their legs only with difficulty. That's when they move to their winter range—the deer yards—sheltered from snow by short, dense needles of hemlock and fir.

Here, the deer spend much of the day "yarded up." Beneath the conifers, they pack down a central resting area where they can stand or lie. They trample pathways in the snow with their hooves so they can easily walk to their favorite feeding areas. When snows are too deep to leave the yard, deer eat the smooth bark off the young hemlock trees. Deer have no front teeth, but strip bark by raking upward with their lower incisors. If you see these one- to two-inch-long tooth marks on small hemlocks, you've probably come upon a deer yard. The scars persist for years.

Porter's studies of radio-collared deer in the Adirondacks showed that deer yards are essentially "owned" by individual family groups, which usually return year after year. A family group may comprise combinations ranging from a single doe and her fawns to up to 20 individuals, including mother, grandmother and sister does, their fawns and male offspring up to 30 months old. Bucks tend to form separate, bachelor herds.

But if snow doesn't get that deep for deer in most northern areas, winter might as well have never come. So they're likely to trade in their yard for yours.

Watch for deer in early morning or at dusk. You might be able to figure out which ones are dominant. An assertive deer will flatten its ears against its neck, lower the head and stare at a subordinate. They also tend to literally step on inferiors.

Arguably the most informative part of the deer is the tail. A deer tends to twitch its tail just before lifting its head. When a deer thinks danger threatens, it erects the white tail like a banner—which is why whitetails are also called "bannertails." This is the signal for the group to bound off, sometimes at speeds greater than 25 miles an hour.

You're particularly likely to get deer visitors if you've planted yew in your yard, one of the deer's favorite foods. You can tell when deer have clipped your hedges because, without upper teeth, they can't cut plants cleanly as rabbits do; instead they grab and pull, leaving ragged edges.

Not everyone is happy to have 300-pound ungulates making their shrubs into topiary. If you want to discourage browsing, try soap. At least that's what orchardists Ken and Peggy McLeod do, dangling motel-size bars from their apple trees. "Apparently, deer don't like the smell," says Peggy McLeod. She reports the family have tested Dial, Safeguard and Ivory brands so far. The deer seem to find them equally offensive.

But if your bushes and trees can use a good pruning, sit back and enjoy the show.

The Ordinary Miracle of Ice

❧

I T'S THREE TIMES TOUGHER THAN GRANITE. Virtually bullet-proof. Stands up to torpedoes better than steel. This is the stuff of which great ships should be made—or so thought Winston Churchill. Yet a child can begin to melt it with a single puff of breath.

If we weren't so preoccupied scraping our windshields, salting our sidewalks and shoveling our driveways, surely we'd consider ice a miracle.

Ice is a shape-shifter, a substance that seems to disobey all the rules. It's nearly always right on the verge of turning into something else: changing from a solid to a liquid, from a liquid to a solid or from a vapor to a solid (which we call snow, but is really a kind of ice crystal). Its convenient freezing point, at 32 degrees F, is precisely what makes ice—literally and figuratively—such a slippery substance. Few other materials we encounter in the natural world exhibit a freezing point at a temperature we can survive.

This freezing point makes ice so changeable it almost acts like a living thing. Ice, after all, grows, as those who have watched their local pond "ice over" well know. Like a living creature, ice can move: traveling much like an ice skater, along a surface lubricated with water melted by friction, some glaciers even "surge" at speeds up to a third of a mile a year. "It's not going to run you over or anything," says Dartmouth College glaciologist William Hibler, "but if there's a village in front of a surging glacier, you've got a problem."

And, like an animal, ice can even leave tracks: on ocean bottoms, scientists have found the "footprints" of icebergs, great trenches carved when these chunks of floating ice scraped against sea sediments.

These aren't the only records of ice's movement on the planet. Much of our landscape was sculpted by glaciers. Ice even "remembers" those times, and beyond: ice cores pulled from deep within glaciers hold trapped air from 100,000 years ago, allowing scientists to study the composition of the Earth's ancient atmosphere and even chart climate changes.

Ice's more recent past is easier to read still. By examining the ice on your local pond, lake or road, you can often tell the conditions under which the ice formed—important information for your immediate future, such as whether that ice is safe to walk or skate on, or a good place to drill a hole to fish for bluegill, trout or pike. But first it helps to understand how Nature manufactures the stuff.

Ice is at once among the world's strangest substances and one of the most common. If it weren't both, says Samuel Colbeck, a geophysicist with the U.S. Army's Cold Regions Research and Engineering Laboratories, "the world as we know it wouldn't exist." Most of the world's fresh water is tied up in the two giant ice sheets covering much of the Arctic and Antarctic. But if ice behaved like most materials, it would sink instead of float. Lakes and seas would freeze from the bottom up and kill all marine life in the process. Fortunately, ice disobeys the grade-school physics lesson that cold contracts materials and heat expands them.

Actually, that rule depends on the matter and the temperature in question. Water expands as it freezes—which is why ice cubes float in your glass: ice is less dense than liquid water. This explains why shore ice along a lake or stream reaches up past what was the water level when the temperature began to drop—in freezing, the upper layers of the water have been pushed up and out.

Water currents cause rivers and streams to freeze more slowly and melt faster than small, still ponds. The friction of these currents generates heat. Protruding stumps and rocks enhance currents; these are signposts to weak spots in the ice. (And they're a good sign fish may lurk nearby, say ice fishermen; oxygen-rich weed beds tend to grow here.) But sometimes you'll see a wet patch on a solidly frozen lake and there's nothing sticking up out of the water. This may well indicate the location of a bottom spring, whose current can keep the water open or slushy for most of the winter. Steer clear!

Sometimes you'll come upon ice so clear it looks like water—you might even see fish swimming beneath your feet. This ice is composed of pure water that froze slowly, eliminating the air bubbles that often make ice look cloudy. Sometimes, because you can see the dark lake bottom through such a covering, this is called black ice; so is the transparent skim of ice on asphalt roads. This kind of ice makes for great skating (which is a problem if you're on tires instead of skates). Ice clouded with impurities, air bubbles or snow offers a bumpier ride.

Even when solidly frozen, ice may undergo another transformation. When temperatures get low enough, ice will finally contract. This causes the booming and cracking you'll hear on really cold days. Although the sound is alarming, you're in no danger. Once thoroughly frozen, ice is incredibly strong. A two-inch-thick sheet of ice can hold up 160 pounds. (Remember, though, that when you take a step, you transfer momentum as well as weight onto the ice. Six inches of ice is a safer measure.)

The strength of ice was one reason why Winston Churchill wanted to make aircraft carriers out of it during World War II. An ice ship would be less vulnerable to U-boat attack than a steel-hulled craft—ice absorbs energy extremely well. Because ice is always so near its melting point, it tends to deform rather than fracture. This explains why glaciers are notoriously difficult to dynamite, and why rescue workers can't hear avalanche victims screaming for help two feet away.

Because ice floats, Churchill's proposed aircraft carrier would be nearly impossible to sink. But best of all for an island nation, an ice ship could be made out of a raw material England possessed in abundance: water.

Churchill was so enthused about the idea he set up a secret study commission to investigate it—probing how beams and sawdust might strengthen the structure, how refrigeration units could be built-in to keep it from melting, how a surface might be prepared so airplanes wouldn't just slide off the ice into the ocean.

Things proved more complicated than Churchill imagined. The project was abandoned mid-war (although some of the leading scientists on that committee later comprised what is now the International Glaciological Society).

But the idea was perhaps no crazier than one floated by Frederick Tudor 100 years earlier: that fortunes could be made by shipping the ice of Walden Pond across the world to cool drinks and make ice cream in Singapore and Calcutta. Although much of the ice melted before reaching its destination, enough of the precious substance made it that by 1855, 12 companies were shipping it out of Boston. Half a world away, a wintertime nuisance was hailed as a miracle, and ice became Boston's leading export.

A Whole Lot of
Hooting Going On

ERIE SCREAMS HAUNT THE CEMETERY. Demonic laughter threads through the pines. Swamps throb with shrieks and catcalls. And from the local woods, the question repeats over and over, as if uttered by a hungry ghost: "Who cooks for you? Who cooks for you? Who cooks for you-all?"

These nighttime voices seem to belong to banshees, demons, maniacs. But they belong to creatures stranger still: night-flying birds with oddly flattened faces, with ears asymmetrically arranged with the right higher than the left, and with eyes so huge that if ours occupied so vast a proportion of our face, our eyes would be as big as oranges. The voices belong to owls, and on February nights, their calls float through the still, cold air like spirits.

"This is definitely the time of year to listen for owls," insists Harris Center conservation educator Janet Altobell. This is the time of year she prowls for owls with second- and third-graders and their families, listening in the local woods in the night.

"Right now there's a whole lot of hooting going on," agrees Wayne Petersen, Massachusetts Audubon ornithologist. In fact, while you may hear the voices of owls any time during the year, late February and early March offer the best chances to catch the duets of two of the most vocal owls in the U.S., the great horned and the barred. Although both species possess a varied repertoire, ranging from hisses to cackles, they're best known for those owl classics: the great horned's deep, mellow "who-hoo-ho-o-o" and the barred owl's "Who cooks for you? Who cooks for you? Who cooks for you-all?" The calls may carry for a mile.

What are these owls really saying? People have been guessing at that for centuries. Thirteenth-century Persians thought the owls were dispensing wisdom. (But hey, they also thought one out of two owl eggs was a hair tonic, and the other egg was a depilatory.) Many other cultures assumed owls foretold doom. (Some folks in Cajun country down in Louisiana still believe hoot owls announce a coming death, which might be warded off by getting up and turning a left shoe upside down. If that doesn't work, it's said that turning a left pocket inside out might do the trick.)

No one has completely decoded owls' cackles, shrieks and hoots. But this time of year, in the most frequently heard vocalizations, owls are saying about the same stuff you find on Valentines. These young owls are selecting mates, and established owl couples—they pair for life—are renewing vows. One owl calls, its mate answers. The larger, more dominant female's voice is usually the louder.

Great horneds are just about to lay their eggs, often in the big abandoned stick nest of a red-tailed hawk in a white pine. Barred owls are getting ready to do so later in March and on into April. As part of their courtship, couples are announcing their territories— lands they may hold for eight years or more. And that is why, if you hoot at owls, they will often answer you, and frequently fly in for a closer look. (And that's why you shouldn't overdo your hoots. Too many foreign hoots could cause an owl to vacate its territory— or to attack you.)

The chance to hear an owl call is a magical opportunity. "It's incredible how many people you can get at three in the morning to go out in the freezing cold to go owling," says Petersen. It's enough to inspire even little kids to stay quiet. When Altobell leads kids on nighttime owl prowls in nearby forests, she says "the noisiest thing about it is the nylon snowsuits rubbing together!"

Any time after dark may yield owl calls, but the best time to go, insists Petersen, is right before first light. Pick a windless night— the owls are more active then, and you will hear better too.

Although most owl species prefer dense woods, any place with

lots of big, old trees *could* harbor an owl—parks, woods, shady backyards, cemeteries. If you're owling for great horneds, visit at night the
sorts of places you'd see red-tailed hawks during the day: broken
terrain, pine woods at the edge of a field. Barred owls (who may hoot
as late as 7 A.M.) prefer hemlock forests and maple swamps.

Although screech owls don't nest till spring, you're likely to hear
them, too, on your midwinter owling expedition. On a good night,
says Petersen, you may hear 15 or 20 screech owls offering up
quavering whistles, descending whinnies or hollow, monotonous
calls. In evergreen forests, you may also hear the voice of the tiny
saw-whet owl, uttering the "skreigh-aw" for which it is named, or a
mechanical tooting call, an upward, slurred whistle or the sound of
a squeaky gate.

Be sure to bring a flashlight when you go owling. If you're quiet,
owls don't mind the light. A full moon adds to the magic but isn't
really necessary to find owls. Their huge eyes—not spherical like
ours but tubular, like binoculars—can gather enough light to hunt
on even pitch-black nights. (Their odd eyes, in fact, cannot move
in their sockets. But no matter: an owl can twist its neck 270 degrees, and snap it around so fast its stare seems continuous.) And
what owls can't see, they can hear. Asymmetrically placed ears and
round, flat faces help gather and pinpoint the faintest mouse squeak,
a job owls accomplish with much acrobatic head-bobbing and body-
rocking. The prey seldom knows what hit it. With wingbeats muf-
fled by its ruffled-edged feathers, the owl floats through the sky,
silent as a moth.

Owls' diets can be quite eclectic. Great horneds have been known
to take prey as prickly as porcupines and as powerful as golden eagles.
New Hampshire Fish and Game biologist Ted Walski says that during particularly snowy winters, with voles and mice hidden beneath
the ice crust, he's found wild turkeys headless in the woods—and he
thinks owls might be the culprits. (Owls often eat the head of the
prey first.)

Owls even eat other owls. A few years back, Diane De Luca,
New Hampshire Audubon senior biologist/ornithologist, used to

hear the calls of both a barred and a great horned owl around her yard in Deering, New Hampshire. Then one day she found a pile of brown barred owl feathers. A few feet away, beneath the red oak by the road where the great horned liked to sit, she found a neat five-inch-long pellet—a compact bundle of indigestible fur, bones, feet and insect parts the owl brings up and spits out after the meal is digested. She didn't actually see what happened, she said, "but the story was pretty clear."

Fox Tracks in Snow

Tales of Intrigue and Ardor

❦

W ENDY VAN DE POLL had hardly shut the door to her truck when she saw the first set of tracks in the snow: a straight row of neat, oval prints, almost like a dotted line, a claw mark showing at the tip of each toe. They were similar to pet dog prints—but bigger dogs leave a messy track, a wider straddle.

The animal who had left these prints weighed only as much as a well-fed house cat, and like a cat, stepped carefully, placing the hind foot precisely inside the track of the front. Here was a creature "so light and wraithlike," in the words of wildlife photographer Leonard Lee Rue III, "that it moves like thistledown blown along by the wind," an animal of legendary wiles and catlike grace: a red fox.

Researching her master's thesis, the young woman followed the tracks, reading their story. The fox had trotted purposefully along the logging road, then entered the woods and stopped to lap from a puddle. Next it had marked a hemlock seedling with the pungent odor of its urine: the three-legged stance confirmed this was a male. Exactly 507 paces from the puddle, Van de Poll saw a second set of tracks, and knew what was on the fox's mind: he was joined by a vixen. Now, the Antioch/New England Graduate School student predicted, things would get really interesting.

As part of her study of wild dogs, Van de Poll has followed wolves in Minnesota and tracked coyotes at The Quabbin Reservoir in Massachusetts. "A wolf or coyote you can track for miles and there's nothing to be seen but traveling," she says. "But foxes are very inquiring. What's exciting and intriguing is all that activity: they'll stop, play around, investigate things. And you can see much of it in a very short space."

In January and February's snows, fox tracks tell stories more vivid than any other North American mammal's. To the novice tracker, following a coyote is as daunting as reading a Proustian tome. But this time of year, fox tracks are the Judith Kranz novels of animal tracking: in them you'll find fast-paced, easy-to-read love stories. In these winter months, fox and vixen flirt and play, cementing and renewing pair-bonds that usually last as long as both survive.

All this is happening nearby. The gray fox, whose tail is tipped in black, sticks to wooded areas. But red foxes live closer to us than most of us realize, preferring suburbs to wilderness, often trotting right through backyards. Tracks, scats or even a glimpse of the fluffy reddish coat and distinctive white-tipped, brushy tail testify to its presence—proof, as Todd Fuller, a carnivore biologist at the University of Massachusetts/Amherst, puts it, "that somebody smart is living right outside the window."

That reputation for cunning is well-deserved. Pursued by hounds and gunmen, a fox will erase its own scent trail by running in streams, walking along railway tracks, trotting over freshly manured, ploughed or burned fields. It will run on thin ice, apparently realizing what will happen to the much heavier hounds in its pursuit. Foxes have also been known to run relays: when one begins to tire of being chased, sometimes its mate will meet it and take over the chore of leading the hounds while the original target hides in a hole.

Although fox pairs spend much of the year apart—they split after their young disperse in autumn—when they are together they are devoted lovers. Van de Poll read the delight of the couple whose tracks joined in the snow: an explosion of tracks told of playful bows and dashes, of moments standing face to face where perhaps wet tongues had caressed each other's muzzles.

FOXES SPEND MUCH OF THE YEAR APART, BUT WHEN
PAIRS MATE, THEY ARE DEVOTED TO EACH OTHER AND
USUALLY REMAIN SO AS LONG AS BOTH SURVIVE.

Meetings between male and female, said photographer Rue, "could only be described with one word—ecstasy." When he was studying a family at their den site in Alaska, "the female almost always saw the male coming before I did," he wrote in his book *The World of the Red Fox*, "but I instantly knew of his approach because the female's body would become taut and she would shiver in anticipation. As the male drew near, the female bounded out to greet him . . . and would flop down on her belly, raise her tail over her back and wave it furiously." Then she would spring up, and kiss him all over with her tongue, and he would do the same. Only then would the reunited couple venture below ground to greet their pups.

Soon, fox pairs will investigate sites for a den in which vixens will bear their 3 to 10 pups in spring. Foxes are good diggers, but often prefer to renovate an existing hole, like the burrow of a woodchuck—whom they evict by eating him.

But as established couples reunite and as young foxes pair up, now is a joyous time to flirt, hunt and play together. (Their appetite for play apparently includes a sense of humor: at a country club outside Philadelphia, one fox would wait for golf balls to land in a certain copse, so it could run out, seize them and dash back to cover.) The two foxes Van de Poll followed romped and played. They paused often to scent-mark their hunting territory, like lovers who carve their names into trees. She could see where one of them had dug in the earth, poked a nose beneath the snow, and pounced on a mound of leaves where perhaps a mouse or vole was hiding.

Here, the fox had leapt high in the air and come down with forepaws perfectly together to pin the prey. Donald and Lillian Stokes, authors of the *Stokes Nature Guides* series, watched the whole sequence as a fox, intent on hunting, came so close to them that, with their binoculars, they could see the slitlike pupils of its eyes.

The fox had first wandered erratically in the field, nose down. At a squeal, ears pricked forward. Another step, and the fox froze, one paw in front. Then it leapt. "After two more quick stabs with its forefeet, it poked its muzzle into the snow and came up emptymouthed," they recalled. A few minutes later the fox found it had also missed something much bigger: the Stokes were standing only 50 feet away. The wind had blown their scent in the opposite direction, and the fox may not have seen the couple because of afternoon glare on the snow. But when it did spot them, it vanished into a hedgerow.

Most foxes prefer to hunt towards evening, at night and at dawn. The tracks Van de Poll followed had likely been left the night before. She nearly lost the trail among a swamp criss-crossed with the triangular back-footprints of snowshoe hare—much smelling and rushing had followed. But then the foxes' trail led away from the swamp and into a hemlock forest.

Here, she found two shallow, fox-shaped depressions surrounded by soft hemlock seedlings. In this cozy bed the two had lain down, side by side, tails curled round their faces like muffs, and perhaps slept till dawn.

Birches in Winter

Ballet of Gaiety and Grace

T
HEIR SUBTLE CURVES glisten white against the straight, dark trunks of other trees. Like playful ballet dancers amid a battalion of straight-backed soldiers, the birches offer cheerful respite from the dark winter woods.

"Oaks for ruggedness and spruce for sober dignity," wrote nature writer Robert Lemmon when he catalogued *The Best Loved Trees of America.* But the birch tribe "has little use for such sober virtues," he asserted. "Gaiety and grace stand high among its assets."

In February, when gaiety and grace may seem in short supply, birches invite us to partake of their delights.

"People love trees you can interact with," says botanist Ty Minton, co-chairman of the Environmental Studies Department at Antioch/New England Graduate School in Keene, New Hampshire. Birches invite interaction: their curling bark draws kids irresistibly to peel it. (Peel once, only the curling part, and you won't hurt the tree. Nothing makes a better fire-starter.) From the leaves of the red birch you can also make a fragrant wintergreen-flavored tea, and from its fast-flowing sap, both pancake syrup and a sparkly, champagnelike beer.

At no time are these trees more balletic than after a February ice storm. Glazed in crystal, their pale, slender forms arch in the woods "like girls on hands and knees that throw their hair/before them over their heads to dry in the sun," as Robert Frost wrote in his poem "Birches."

Ice storms that tear the limbs from other trees only make birches more beautiful. Swinging on birches in summertime, as Frost suggests in his poem, doesn't permanently bow them, but ice storms may. If a storm lasts several days, the tree will never recover its original posture.

Perhaps this is why, when the American Forestry Association founded a movement to plant trees on Mother's Day, the first tree set forth to honor mothers of the nation was a white birch—an apt symbol for the flexibility and sacrifice that motherhood demands.

And perhaps it is this combination of poignancy and gaiety that moves so many poets to celebrate the feminine charms of the birches. Samuel Coleridge called the English birch "the lady of the woods." Henry Wadsworth Longfellow begged the paper birch to give its bark; with it, he vowed to build a canoe "that shall float upon the river/like a yellow leaf in Autumn/like a yellow water lily." James Russell Lowell considered the gray birch (probably the same species Frost swung upon) a tree of such ladylike delicacy that "thy shadow scarce seems shade."

Yet the birches were sculpted by forces tough as granite and ruthless as hail. Birches' flexibility, as well as their distinctive light-colored, peeling bark, are adaptations to the extremes of northern winters.

Although the river birch may be found below the Mason-Dixon line, birches evolved in the North, and as a group remain cold-loving creatures. In many areas, they are the main deciduous trees in forests dominated by spruce and fir. The evergreens shed snow and ice from needlelike leaves, but most deciduous trees would be felled by the weight of the heavy snows in the mountains of the Far North. The balletic birches, with no way to shun the snow, survive by yielding to it instead. They bend rather than snap.

Birches can survive as far north as the High Arctic, where they grow only two inches tall on granite outcroppings. The real danger to trees in such frigid climes is not cold, but heat. Dark-colored bark absorbs the heat of sunny winter days; come nightfall, plummeting temperatures can contract smooth bark fast enough to crack it open. Most other trees developed vertically furrowed bark, which functions like an accordion file, to accommodate these extremes. But the smooth-barked birches adopted a different strategy: their light color reflects heat rather than absorbs it.

Maintaining this light color may be the reason birch bark perpetually peels. Antioch ecologist Tom Wessels notes that by regularly shedding their skins, birch trees may prevent the accumulation of lichens, mosses and fungi, which would darken the bark. (The longest-lived of the tribe, the yellow birch, is also the most enthusiastic peeler: among misty, moss-hung forests, it's the only tree that looks like it has eczema.)

Birches' unusual bark makes it ideal for many human uses. The word "birch" derives from the Sanskrit *bhurga*, "a tree whose bark is used for writing upon."

The paper birch was the deciduous tree most often used in the technology of the northern Native Americans, according to horticultural research archivist Sheila Connor, of the Arnold Arboretum. Resinous and flexible, sheets of the waxy, lustrous bark were pulled each spring from the tree by applying heated water to the trunk. Bound with cedar rootlets to springy cedar or spruce frames, the seams and needle holes sealed with pitch, the bark of the paper birch provided the finest canoe covering the wilderness could offer. Native Americans made bowls and built tents from it. They rolled it into megaphones to call bull moose. They even used it to construct coffins.

And the birches' utility runs more than skin deep. Their bite may be more fun than their bark—if you make beer from the sap of the black birch, that is. (The stuff has "the kick of a mule," says Minton. And Wessels still has corks stuck in the sheet rock of his basement from a particularly bubbly batch that burst.) A few weeks after maple sugaring, you can reuse the same equipment to tap the swifter-flowing sap of this fragrant tree. (Euell Gibbons supplies recipes for both beer and syrup in *Stalking the Wild Asparagus*.)

Wintergreen-flavored tea can be made by steeping finely minced twigs in boiling water. Early settlers thought the drink cured dropsy and dissolved kidney stones.

But thanks in no small part to Frost's poem, the most celebrated use of birches remains the province of country boys and girls. The pastime also provides a great incentive for proper botanizing. A student at Vermont's Putney School, fancying himself "a swinger of birches," climbed up a slender trunk—which promptly snapped and crashed to the ground. A broken leg reinforced the lesson: if you're going to swing, choose a birch, not an aspen.

Cannibal Athletes

They Leap Tall Buildings in a Single Bound—
and Then Eat Each Other

O N A WARM DAY IN WINTER, when the ice is no good for skating and the woods are too slushy to ski, when it seems there's nothing to do outside but watch the dirty snow melt—go out and watch the dirty snow melt.

What looks like bits of soot or dirt on melting snow sometimes hops around. If you look closely at these jumping specks, you'll be face to face with tiny creatures so mystifying that specialists are still arguing over what they are.

They are commonly called snow fleas, even though they are not fleas at all but members of a group of six-legged animals called springtails, which may or may not be insects.

Springtails are creatures of paradox. Although each one is less than one-sixteenth of an inch long, they're capable of jumping as far as six inches in a single bound—a feat so impressive that it is as if a man could cover a mile in nine or ten bounds.

Although most people never see springtails except on snow, they live in every habitat except the open ocean, and they are found in some tide pools too. They are among the most prolific and numerous animals on Earth—despite the fact that males and females cannot tell each other apart.

A winter thaw may bring snow fleas out by the millions. Henry David Thoreau observed them in Walden's woods. "The snow flea seems to be a creature whose summer and prime of life is a thaw in the winter," he wrote in his journal on a January day in 1860. "It seems not merely to enjoy this interval like other animals, but then chiefly to exist. That thaw which merely excites the cock to sound his clarion, as it were, calls to life the snow flea."

Charles Mcnamara, a layman springtail enthusiast from Ontario, has seen vast swarms of them blacken the snow. "In hollows and depressions in the snow, such as footprints, from which they cannot readily escape," he wrote in the *Annual Review of Entomology*, "they sometimes accumulate in solid masses that could be ladled out with a spoon."

Sometimes snow fleas emerge in unbelievable numbers. In Switzerland they've been known to stop trains when the rails become slippery with their tiny squashed corpses. In 1993, folks out in Idaho were worried that a chemical spill had occurred on a highway because the tarmac was thick with black powder. The clean-up team discovered it was not toxic waste, but snow fleas.

Not every thaw brings out these small creatures, and some years you won't see any snow fleas at all. Even after decades of studying the animals, biology professor Kenneth Christiansen of Grinnell College in Iowa, a world expert on springtails, is still puzzled about how they decide when to come out. "On a nice, warm, sunny day, suddenly they start boiling up out of the snow," he says, "like people all packed in a subway and somebody yells, 'Fire!'"

Rather than fleeing fire, snow fleas are probably running from too many other snow fleas, Christiansen suspects. Normally they live in leaf litter, eating detritus and breeding enthusiastically.

But if too much of this goes on, leaf litter can get mighty crowded. Howard Ensign Evans, in his book *Life on a Little-Known Planet*, reports that one research outfit started with 10 springtails and eight and a half weeks later had 3,447. This talent for breeding is all the more spectacular when you consider that these creatures never actually mate. Like most springtails, male snow fleas merely dribble bits of semen around the place, and the females just seem to blunder into them.

Casual though it may be, this arrangement works well enough. "It seems perfectly safe to say that springtails are by far the most abundant six-legged animals on the land masses of the Earth, and the most abundant of all animals on land having any legs at all with the probable exception of mites," writes Evans. "He who would prove me wrong had better start counting!"

Biology professor Peter Bellinger of California State University has done so—and agrees with Evans. Collecting springtails from soils beneath pine stands at his study site in Connecticut, Bellinger once counted 6,000 of them in a space less than one foot square. In the Arctic, more than 5,000 have been counted in a six-cubic-inch sample.

Not only are there lots of springtails, there are lots of kinds of springtails and not all of them come out on the snow. Unfortunately, you can't tell them apart with the naked eye because they all just look like specks. So springtail enthusiasts use magnifications of 500 to 1,000 times to study them in their labs. Those you most often see in North America are called *Hypogastrura nivicola*.

In winter, cold-tolerant springtails fare much better than the ants, beetles and birds who eat them. Breeding so prolifically, their numbers increase until they erupt from the ground, climbing out onto the snow and filling small spaces around the stems of weeds and shrubs.

What do they do once they get out? They hop around a lot, using the apparatus for which springtails are named. Near the rear of the abdomen (the "tail") is the "spring"—a forked organ which reaches forward, almost to . . . well, almost to where the chest would be if springtails had chests. Here, the spring is held in place by a catch, like the clasp on a brooch. The catch is a small projection with two sets of teeth that hook onto the inner sides. When the creature activates the muscles that release the catch, the springtail catapults into space.

Entomologist Bellinger notes that a springtail can refasten its clasp and spring anew in less than a second. He once watched one that fell on its back and flipped its spring three times before it righted itself.

The spring comes in handy, as it turns out, in a variety of situations. New evidence shows some species may also use this mechanism to migrate. A paper presented at a recent meeting of entomologists in Helsinki offered observations that a European species, *Hypogastrura socialis*, appears to move en masse almost 1,000 feet a day.

Other evidence suggests that snow fleas might do better if they just stayed underground. Snow fleas seem to spend most of their time on the surface of the snow doing one of two things: trying to get back beneath the snow, and eating each other.

British entomologist W.M. Davies watched a swarm of them under a microscope and found "individuals vigorously attacking other members of the swarm . . . . During an attack, the victim struggled and fought with mouthparts and tarsal claws, but was gradually overpowered." Even the victors are losers in these encounters. The blood of springtails is toxic, and the cannibals are poisoned. ("These are not brilliant animals," remarked Bellinger.)

But then again, given current theories that overpopulation causes springtail swarming, it would seem this all works out rather neatly after all.

Spring

Phantoms
of the Woods

🐌

THE GENTLEMAN HAD PHONED the Massachusetts Division of Fisheries and Wildlife with great excitement. "You're not going to believe this," he told the switchboard operator, "but I've just seen a kangaroo out my window."

Tom French, assistant director of the Natural Heritage and Endangered Species Program, had heard it all before: the Asian pit vipers that turned out to be garter snakes, the black panther that was really the neighbor's house cat backlit by the morning sun.

Of course it wasn't a kangaroo.

It was a wallaby.

Kangaroos can grow to four and a half feet tall. Wallabies—one of the 50 or so Australian variations on the kangaroo theme—are much shorter. This animal was two and a half feet tall, jumped around on its hind feet, and at least 12 people reported it hopping around the streets and yards of Acton, Foxboro and Concord, Massachusetts, in 1989. In other words, several continents beyond its usual range.

This isn't the first time such a thing has happened. Other strange sightings have included an armadillo scuttling around an East Coast office and a flamingo in a pond in Vermont.

It could be cabin fever. But there is another explanation for these phantoms of the woods: "You really can be seeing what you think you're seeing," says Eric Orff, a wildlife biologist with the New Hampshire Fish and Game Department.

True, Orff also got a call from a police chief who said he had seen a Yeti, which Orff doesn't believe. But between escaped zoo animals, unwanted pets and creatures undertaking pilgrimages we don't understand, it's possible to see almost anything in your backyard.

According to French, "most of the more interesting, real records occur at the end of the winter, beginning of spring—right about now." In March, storms blow through bearing strange birds, visibility is good because the trees are bare, and animals everywhere are on the move.

By the way, that wasn't the first wallaby reported in the Boston area in recent years—nor was it the last. Oddest of all, in only one instance could authorities match the wandering wallaby to a known case of a missing marsupial: Aardu, an 18-month-old male Bennett wallaby, escaped from Boston's Stoneham Zoo in July of 1990 and was spotted repeatedly by residents of Malden, Melrose, Medford, Stoneham and Winchester during his 11-day hopping spree until his safe recapture August 3. But there were other wallaby sightings reported in the towns of Southwick and Springfield that August, according to French, and an earlier one reported in Belchertown in the 1970s. These were, says French, "reliable" sightings, reported in accurate detail by multiple, independent sources. And like the Acton wallaby of 1989, no one ever figured out where these animals came from, or where they eventually went.

The wallabies were for real, French believes, and not cases of mistaken identity. But people do make mistakes. Recently, a lady from Cape Cod called the state Fisheries and Wildlife office to report she had found a dead bald eagle on the beach. Since this is an endangered bird seldom seen in Massachusetts, French persuaded her to collect the corpse, bring it back to the house and then describe it to him on the phone.

"Can you tell me what its head looks like?" he asked.

"It's got a big white head," she answered.

"And its beak?"

"It's got a big curved yellow beak," the lady said.

"What color is its body?"

"It's got a black body," she reported.

All these are indeed characteristic of adult bald eagles. French thought a moment. He asked one more question:

"Does it have webbed feet?"

"Yes," responded the lady enthusiastically, "it has the webbed feet."

It was a black-backed gull.

Identifying birds can be confusing. A lot of reported hawks turn out to be ruffed grouse. Both are big birds with banded tails, big talons and curved bills. (Although it might seem more exciting to have found a bird of prey, if it turns out to be a dead grouse, you can eat it.)

"Some of the weird things people see are regular animals in varying degrees of hairiness," says Orff. Mange can transform a fluffy fox into an unidentified cat; with its winter coat fluffed up, a skunk can appear as big as a 50-pound wolverine.

One of the most common errors people make when describing an unknown wild animal is making it bigger than it really is. Minutes after Vermont's Fish and Wildlife Department released some martins, little red tree-dwelling weasels who had become extinct in the state, a passerby spotted one of them. He reported "a thing the size of a cocker spaniel with a long tail," said Steve Parren, coordinator for the Department's NonGame and Natural Heritage Program. The martin, Parren added, "was actually about the size of a squirrel." (To gauge a creature's size accurately, try to note where it measures up to a bush, tree or fence it may be standing near, and then go measure that object.)

In the eyes of the public, many creatures not only grow larger, but also become more exotic. "Unfortunately we get our nature education through television," says French, "and we tend to see the characters we see on TV in our backyards." So Easterners tend to phone in insisting they've seen a badger, a big, western hole-digging weasel, when they've really got a woodchuck. One Massachusetts resident reported he had an armadillo in his yard. It was actually a possum.

But it *could* have been an armadillo. That's what ran into Mark

Pokras's office one wintry day. A horse had come in from Florida for treatment at the veterinary clinic at Tufts University, where Pokras is an assistant professor of wildlife medicine. When the walkway from the horse trailer was lowered, out came the armadillo.

Exotic birds may also make long trips, blowing in with storms—the way Dorothy arrived in the land of Oz. That's how Vermont authorities account for the flamingo that appeared in the summer of 1980 at the mouth of the Winooski River, where it flows into Lake Champlain.

And a lot of odd creatures—and this probably includes the unexplained wallabies—are likely pets people bought impetuously, sometimes illegally, and later just released. This occurs frequently with reptiles, particularly bad-mannered ones, such as the four-foot-long Savannah monitor that was discovered walking along a sidewalk in Worcester, Massachusetts, by a dog officer a few years ago. Although a sleek, handsome creature, light tan with yellow speckles, as a pet the Savannah monitor has its drawbacks. "This is a nasty, nasty lizard with lots of sharp teeth," Pokras explains. "They bite you. They thrash their heads around like a shark and it really hurts." Tufts has recovered as many as six loose Savannah monitors in a given year. When one is captured, a veterinary student usually adopts it as a pet.

Not all phantoms are wayward pets or unwitting vagabonds. Some turn up on purpose, sometimes through efforts that seem heroic.

Until the early 1990s, lynx had not been positively identified in southern New England since the 1800s. About the size of the more common bobcat, the buff-colored, short-tailed lynx, with its distinctive triangular ears tipped with tufts of black hair, has been so widely hunted that it's been almost exterminated from the United States. The only large American populations survive in Alaska, Montana, Idaho and Washington.

In an effort to reintroduce lynx to the region, in 1988 and 1989 New York State biologists released wild-caught, radio-collared lynx from Alaska and the Yukon into the Adirondack wilderness. Some of them reached Massachusetts, Vermont, New Hampshire and even Pennsylvania. In all these states, lynx have been positively identified—unfortunately because wildlife authorities examined the corpses. One was killed by a car in Pennsylvania; three were shot while raiding chicken coops. Two of the animals were wearing radio collars. There could well be other lynx in surrounding areas, undiscovered, phantoms of the woods.

The Mysterious
Partnership
of the Lichen

S PRINGTIME, THE POETS SAY, is a state of mind. After months
of snow, sleet, ice and ugly brown puddles, springtime feels
like a state of desperation—a frantic longing for something
new and fresh and green.

Yet even when most blooms are weeks away, there's plenty of new
growth out there. We need only look in the right places.

Don't look at the tips of the trees—look at the crevices in the
bark. Don't look in the flowerbed—look on the rocks around it.
Look on bricks, gravestones, tile rooftops, logs. For tiny creatures
called lichens, springtime is now in full swing. Even before the
snow has melted, lichens bloom with abandon.

Well, sort of. They don't actually bloom; they don't have flowers.
Or leaves, or roots, for that matter. But lichens do offer a profusion
of colors and shapes. Some look like miniature golf tees, goblets,
candlesticks, lily pads. Some look like moss or tiny corals. Some look
like the little trees decorating model railroads and architectural mod-
els (which are, actually, lichens), and some look like a skin disease
(they aren't—and they don't hurt the trees they grow on). Some are
red, some yellow, some apple-green; others are brown, black, orange,
aqua. At winter's end, thriving in the cool, soaking up snowmelt and
the first rays of springtime sun, lichens have colors more vivid than
at any other time of year.

"On a cloudy day, they start to *glow*," says Katrina Maloney, a lichen enthusiast who teaches biology labs at Franklin Pierce College in Rindge, New Hampshire. Along little-trafficked roadsides, dinner-plate-sized patches of *Parmelia caperata* are turning bright apple-green. Clinging to boulders, lily-pad-shaped *Umbilicaria* lichens change, chameleonlike, from brown to bright green in the rain. Atop fences, stumps and acidic soils, tiny gray-green stalks stand as if at attention, capped with bright red, earning them the common name of British soldier lichen.

Although surely you've seen lichens, perhaps you didn't know what they were. You're in excellent company. Even lichenologists aren't sure. These scientists can't decide whether the creatures they study belong in the Plant Kingdom with trees, flowers and algae, or in the Fungi Kingdom with mushrooms and molds. That's because lichens are both. As David H. Richardson, dean of science at St. Mary's University in Halifax, puts it, each lichen is "a fungal sandwich" with a layer of algae in the middle. Or as Clark University biologist Vernon Ahmadjian explains in *The Lichen Symbiosis*, lichens are "a sophisticated form of parasitism"—fungi that keep algae as slaves.

That each lichen is actually a dual organism is a notion so bizarre that as late as 1953, some scientists were writing papers to discredit it. (Beatrix Potter was among those to support the idea in a paper she submitted to England's Royal Botanical Society. The editors pretty much told her to go back to painting bunnies.)

But it's all plain to see under the microscope. The fungus provides structural support for the alga, like a trellis for a vine. The fungus absorbs nutrients from air and rainwater and shares these with the alga. But the alga does the hard work of photosynthesis for both, using sunlight to make food out of carbon dioxide and water.

Scientists who have taken a lichen and separated its fungus from its alga in a laboratory to culture each separately found that both critters did fine on their own. But put back together again, the original lichen rarely forms. Lichens are almost impossible to propagate in the greenhouse, and arborists almost never succeed in transplanting them. The natural formation of the lichens' strange partnership is "one of the great mysteries of biology," according to Alberta-based lichenologist Janet Marsh.

Mysterious but successful: about 20,000 species of lichen thrive around the world, from sea level to the tops of high mountains, from the Arctic to the Tropics. On a single tree branch, in the space of a foot and a half, you may be able to find five or six species, each incredibly different and beautiful. Lichens cover more of the Earth's surface than do tropical rainforests, Ahmadjian points out—a full 8 percent of the globe. "Many people overlook lichens," he says, "because they think lichens are small and insignificant, but they're not."

Far from insignificant, lichens provide dyes and medicines, fixatives for perfumes and flavorings for foods. Nine thousand tons of two species of lichen, misnamed oak moss and tree moss, are harvested from North Africa's Atlas Mountains, central France and the lands of former Yugoslavia each year. Baled up like hay, they're shipped to Grasse, the perfume capital of the world, in southern France, to act as fixatives to keep fine perfume subtly fragrant.

Scandinavia harvests another 2,000 tons of reindeer lichen to adorn the graves of Central European dead. (Unlike cut flowers, lichens don't wilt.) In India, so many lichens are used to flavor masalas and curries that many species there are becoming rare.

Until quite recently, lichens yielded the dye for Harris tweed—conferring not only a distinctive color, but also moth-proofing the wool. Rock-growing lichens also provided one of the key ingredients for a royal purple dye used widely in Europe until the mid-1800s, when easier processes were discovered. (The other key ingredient, Richardson notes, was ammonia, which was derived from human urine. Urine carts would visit city neighborhoods daily, assiduously avoiding the homes of known beer-drinkers, who yielded a product considered "impure." After fermenting with the lichens for weeks, the resulting dye was said to smell like violets.)

Lichens are also a source of natural antibiotics. Lichens live long (Arctic moraines support lichens 4,000 years old) and grow slowly. To repel invasion by microbes and insects, they have evolved an array of chemicals, some of which fend off human ailments as well.

Antibiotic pastilles made from a lichen called Iceland moss are sold over the counter in Scandinavia to cure sore throats; another species is used to kill bacteria in the natural deodorants made by Tom's of Maine.

But perhaps lichens are most important to us for the warnings they provide. Because they absorb all their nutrients directly from air and rainwater, monitoring the presence or absence, size and health of lichens can detect, measure and map pollution. For this reason, Richardson calls *Parmelia caperata* the "30 miles per hour lichen"; along roads with higher speed limits and more traffic, these apple-green lichens disappear, unable to survive the car fumes.

Lots of healthy lichens mean clean water and air. Richardson likes to close his lichen lectures exhorting his audience to work to achieve what he terms the rallying call of environmentalists:

"Air fit for lichens and water fit for trout."

The Beloved Robin's
Alter Ego

I REMEMBER ONE LONG WINTER in the country when it seemed that spring would never come," author Florence A. Merriam wrote in 1898. "At last one day the call of a robin rang out . . . . When they come back, what good cheer they bring with them!"

Such good cheer, indeed, that many field guides report that the robin is caroling these words:

"Cheer-up, Cheerily,
Cheer-up, Cheer-up, cheerily!"

But wait—is this *really* what the robins are saying?

Grace Archibald of Winchester, Massachusetts, reports robins are sounding a warning:

"Captain Gillet, Captain Gillet,
Get your skillet, get your skillet!
It's going to ra-in!"

Betty Treiber, a bird-listener in Alexandria, Virginia, says they are shouting out good news:

"The cherries are ripe!
The cherries are ripe!"

The respected author and ornithologist Edward Howe Forbush found the words to the robin's "well-known carol" were far more ominous. In his 1925 classic, *A Natural History of American Birds*, Forbush insisted that the robin's words were more like "Kill 'em, cure 'em, give 'em physic."

Even though the robin's song lasts from dawn to dusk and begins within days of his reappearance each spring, even though he sings the song all summer, and even though human beings have been listening to robin song for at least as long as North America has been inhabited—we still aren't agreed on the lyrics.

The most extensive translation was offered in 1923 by a Dr. Leroy Titus Weeks. He claimed the robin was clearly saying:

"Pillywink, pollywog, poodle, poodle,
Pollywog, poodle, pillywink, pillywink,
Poodle, poodle, pillywink, pollywog,
Poodle, poodle."

The argument over the robin's song is not the only clue that we don't know these familiar creatures as well as we think we do. First migrants of spring? Maybe not. Many of the robins you're just now seeing in your yard have been here all winter long. America's most beloved bird? Maybe up North they are, but in some quarters down South they're despised as agricultural pests—a sin for which, a century ago, they were routinely shot by the thousands. ("They are fat and juicy and afford excellent eating," reported no less an ornithological authority than John James Audubon, who frequently dined on his study subjects.)

Agricultural pests? The worm-eating, lawn-loving robin? The very same. But in winter, robins dramatically change their behavior. They congregate in flocks of up to 50,000, and rather than hunt worms, they eat fruit, often destroying much of an orchardist's crops.

"It's as if robins have two different personalities," says Wayne Petersen, field ornithologist for the Massachusetts Audubon Society.

Even its name is a case of mistaken identity. British settlers called our American redbreast by the same name as their European robin—a bird which ours doesn't particularly resemble and to which it isn't even related. (Their robin looks like a bluebird. Ours is more closely related to the European blackbird, which, like our robin, is a kind of thrush.)

Why call it a robin at all? Because, like the European original, the male American robin's devotion and ardor reminded the settlers of love-struck teenagers, who were called robins in medieval

IT TAKES ROBINS FIVE TO SIX 12-HOUR DAYS
TO BUILD A NEST, BUT NESTLINGS ARE EVEN MORE
WORK—EACH NEEDS 14 FEET OF WORMS A DAY.

England. Which, as it turns out, was also an error—or at least, only partially true.

"Robins are landowners first and lovers only second," asserts animal behaviorist Len Eiserer. In his book *The American Robin*, Eiserer explains that the male is more attached to his territory than to his spouse—and the feeling is mutual. Only one in eight robins takes up with a mate of past years, the author reports, while more than half of all robins return to the same neighborhood as the previous year.

Reclaiming these beloved territories is what the songs are all about. Each territory comprises about half an acre, often bounded by some topological feature like the hedgerow that separates your yard from your neighbor's.

Robins defend their land against all invaders: other male robins, but also squirrels, cats, dogs and even formidable hawks and owls. But, like people, robins also congregate on common ground. Sometimes you'll see gatherings of dozens of robins, zig-zagging around, fishing for worms on ballfields, lawns and golf courses. There are two reasons for this zig-zagging. One, with their eyes on opposite sides of their head, this is the best position to look for worms, who tend to nap with their tails protruding slightly from their burrows. And two, the very sight of a robin's red breast head-on could provoke another robin to attack him. (This urge is irresistible. One March, a Kansas City robin was reported to have skirmished with his reflection in a window for 16 days.)

Once a territory is established, robins settle down, often building their mud-lined nests on eaves and porches, and there play out a scene of domestic bliss to an approving human audience. Except for eating worms, they do things much as we like to think we do: the devoted husband and wife work hard to build a nice home in the suburbs and raise the kids. And hard work it is: a typical nest requires 500 to 600 flights to ferry construction materials, and takes five or six 12-hour days to build. The nestlings are even more work: each baby needs to eat 14 feet of worms a day!

For reflecting our own family values, perhaps no other northern-nesting bird is so beloved, or inspires more fervent devotion. A robin felled by a schoolboy's stone in Wisconsin was nursed by police and, come fall migration, rushed to Jacksonville, Florida, by train. Another, disabled by cat attack, was doctored by a florist and then, when it recovered in late fall, flown to Miami on Eastern Airlines (which offered a discounted bird ticket for $6.36).

No northerner wants to see a robin miss the trip south. But, while it's true that many robins migrate—indeed, ribbons of migrating robins stretching 10 miles wide have been recorded—many don't fly south at all.

"A lot of folks don't realize the number of robins around in winter," says Wayne Petersen. One recent winter, Massachusetts' Christmas Bird Count tallied more than 11,000 robins along one 15-mile swath of land between Massachusetts and Rhode Island alone.

If robins stay the winter, why don't we see them? Because winter robins don't act like the redbreasts of spring and summer. They don't carol. They don't hunt worms. They don't frequent dooryards or porches. Come cold weather, these friendly suburban birds turn into shy forest denizens, fearful of humans. They gather in immense flocks in woods and swamps, feasting on red cedar and holly berries.

And perhaps even more surprising, robins flock even in spring and summer—though we seldom see it. After dusk, the solicitous husband and father robin often leaves wife and children at the nest, and goes to a bachelor roost in the woods. We wake to find him where we last saw him—beside his mate, among his offspring—because he returns to join his family right before dawn.

Early Spring's Subtle Splendors

꧁

S PRING, AS ITS NAME IMPLIES, has the reputation of a sudden season: a change of scenery from winter's frozen landscape quick as time-lapse photography. Although spring has "sprung" in song and poetry ever since Ovid's *Metamorphosis* in 66 A.D., up North we know differently. "Spring moves north at a saunter," naturalists Ed Duensing and A.B. Millmoss tell us in their book *The Backyard and Beyond*—it's heading toward us at about 13 miles a day, by their calculations.

Some springs, though, seem more like a schlep than a saunter. We seem to be stuck in a kind of demi-season, a wet, gray desert of melting snow and dead grass and mud puddles. But look again: the signs of spring are here, all right; they just aren't terribly obvious. You have to hunt them out—which makes finding them all the more rewarding.

"If you're walking around and look closely," says Ted Elliman, education director of the New England Wild Flower Society, "you'll see all these different colors, subtle and beautiful: shades of red and yellow, delicate green leaves emerging from buds."

Early spring's subtle splendors often occur in forms and in places you might never expect. Most of the earliest flowers are not found on the ground. Many of the blossoms have no petals. And some of the most stunning blooms are no bigger than the head of a dressmaker's pin. "If people were more aware of the subtleties of plants," says Barbara Pryor, the Society's public relations director, "they wouldn't find this time of year so stark."

The first ground-dwelling plant to flower does not look like a flower, does not act like a plant and doesn't smell like a bouquet. It's the flower of the skunk cabbage, and you can see it growing now in snow-bound swampy woods: a flame-shaped magenta and lime "spathe" shields a pale yellow pineapplelike flower bud (an arrangement much like the jack-in-the-pulpit flower).

You will find the snow around the flower has melted, for this plant dramatically alters its own environment by generating heat. The heat is produced by the respiration of the plant, reminding one of a person warming his hands with his own breath. If you touch the flower, it will feel warm—it maintains a fairly constant temperature of 70 degrees F. But if you touch it too roughly, you may also get another, less pleasant sensation: a scent that naturalist-authors Don and Lillian Stokes describe as "a mixture of rubber tires and garlic." (The odor probably attracts flies to pollinate the plant.)

For more surprises, look up: most people don't realize that trees flower. Yet, Pryor points out, most of the first plants to flower in the spring are trees and shrubs.

Spicebush, which grows at the edges of swamps, often near skunk cabbage, is now in bloom, putting forth tufts of tiny yellow flowers, exuding a lemon fragrance. Hazelnut is also blooming—but because the flowers are so small and so early, most people miss them entirely.

That's a situation Elliman would like to correct, because this is one of his favorite flowers: a blazing jewel of bright crimson, tiny as a dot, delicate as a tuft of thread. It lacks most of the parts of "normal" flowers: it has no petals or sepals (the green part at the base of flowers like daisies). It's entirely composed of seven or eight hair-like pistils—the female organs of the flower—which extend from the tip of the branch. You'll see hazelnuts flowering in uplands, often in the understory of older forests, in clearings or along woodland borders.

Some of the most dramatic spring blooms belong to the red maple. This widespread tree is named not for its fall foliage—which can range from purple to red to yellow—but for its bright red spring flowers. Red maples grow on acid soils, from rocky hillsides to swamps, often in association with yellow birch. In early spring, their branches seem to glow, as if lit from within. The blooms cluster at the tips of the tree's branches and will stay open for weeks on slender, two-inch stalks.

Some of spring's earliest flowers look so unlike flowers that they go by a different name. When minute, petalless flowers grow in long, drooping clusters—like on willows, aspens, birches and oaks—they are called "catkins." The name comes from *kattekin*, the now-obsolete Dutch word for "little cat," because they look like kittens' tails. The best-known, and best-loved, of these are pussy willows, which you'll find along stream banks, near marshes, even planted as ornamentals in backyards. The fuzz on the pussy willow protects the flower and keeps it warm like a woolly sweater. Later in the season, you'll see the silver catkin gilded with yellow pollen.

You can even enjoy flowers—and leaves—long before they open. Buds are often colorful, always beautiful structures: The beech sports long, dagger-pointed yellow leaf buds. Yellow birch has handsome bronze-colored buds that are somewhat hairy; break them off and you'll smell a wintergreen scent. Basswood's bright red leaf buds are edible; deer like them, and so does Elliman (warning: he also enjoys okra, which has a similar texture). Oak leaf buds are pinkish red, and the emerging leaves, also pinkish, look like flowers.

Flower buds are larger than leaf buds, and often flower buds are at the tip of a branch. Few people realize that these structures form in the autumn and stay on the tree or bush all winter, usually covered with protective scales. A bud is actually the furled-up adult leaf or flower in miniature—like a homunculus: a promise about to be fulfilled.

The Blackfly

Vampire with a Boxer's Face

PEOPLE UP HERE ARE SO FRIENDLY," one Southern visitor commented, after driving up to New Hampshire for the first time one May. No stand-offish New Englanders here, he concluded. "They even wave at your car as you drive past!"

Not to disappoint spring visitors, but those people aren't waving. They're trying to shoo away blackflies.

No run-of-the mill houseflies, these. Blackflies form dense clouds around your head, much like midges and gnats. But unlike those delicate, fragile-looking insects, blackflies are strong and compact. And another thing: they bite, usually leaving behind welts that bleed, itch and swell.

Cities are relatively free of blackflies. Their wormlike larvae live only in clean, fast-flowing streams and rivers—the very waterways that draw city folk to northern rural villages, mountain resorts and fishing lodges. What the brochures don't report is that more than 40 species of blackflies begin to emerge from these waterways in late April, reaching a silent crescendo in May. Travel further north, into Canada, and you'll find a second and third wave of blackflies hatching, on into June, July and even August.

Rather, they'll find you. Attracted to the carbon dioxide in your breath, clouds of these broad-winged, quarter-inch-long flies mill about your face and fly into your nose, ears and eyes. Which is why University of New Hampshire blackfly expert Dr. John Burger, not a vain person, carries a mirror with him all spring—to help him fish blackfly corpses out of his eyes.

"It's hard to find any human being who has a good word to say about blackflies," writes Sue Hubbell in her book on bugs, *Broadsides from the Other Orders.* "Blackflies," she writes, "are Bad Bugs."

How bad? So bad that some historians think blackflies might have caused the spring migrations of many tribes of Native Americans—to get away from the swarms. Out in peninsular Michigan, there's a golf tournament called the Black Fly Open. Says blackfly expert Richard Merrit, an entomologist at Michigan State University, the swarms are so thick "people try to hit the golf ball and they can't even see it."

Blackflies don't torment only people. Of the world's 1,154 known species, most won't bite us at all—one kind only drinks blood from loons. Many species attack livestock, and the beleaguered beasts may lose enough blood and foraging time to do them in. During the blackfly plague year of 1923 in Yugoslavia, Rumania and Bulgaria, 20,000 horses, cattle, sheep and goats are said to have died from the depredations of blackflies.

Ready for more bad news? They're going to get worse. According to John D. Edman, an entomologist at the University of Massachusetts, pollution from logging and industry drove many species away from northern rivers. The larvae, wormlike critters filtering detritus from the water with "head fans" in front of their mouths, attach themselves to rocks and leaves in clear, fast-running water; later they pupate, like butterflies, and then hatch out as flies. "Now," he says, "as water quality is increasing, they're reclaiming their range." Poor water quality meant that, for the past few decades, many areas' worst blackfly species bred in small, sometimes temporary streams—and the bulk of them were gone by Father's Day. Cleaner rivers mean better habitat for the species that hatch out all summer long.

But you've got to admire the creatures, even while swatting at them. One look at a blackfly's pugilist face (the family name in Latin means "little snub-nosed beings") and you can see this is one tough cookie. They can fly more than 200 miles. They've persisted unchanged for 180 million years. And that's thanks, in part, to an array of jaws like a set of Ginsu knives and an arsenal of chemicals that make them blood suckers extraordinaire.

Like mosquitoes, which are also flies, only the females bite. They need blood to lay their eggs, and they may bite only once, twice or possibly thrice in their lives—but that's more than enough for most people.

"These things are little vampires," says entomologist Ed Cupp. If you can stand it, he advises, watch a blackfly as she selects you as her victim: first she hovers, watching and scenting. Then she alights. She pats your skin with her front legs. On her front feet are sense organs that help her decide whether to bite or not.

What happens next you'd need a microscope to see. First the fly clamps on with a set of teeth in the front of her mouth. Two rows of teeth behind those saw through your skin to create a little pool of blood. While the insect sucks that up, the blackfly lowers yet another set of mouthparts through which she pumps saliva into the wound. This is why blackfly bites bleed so much, itch so badly and why Cupp works at the Black Fly Research Laboratory at the University of Arizona. There, he is investigating the recipe for black-fly drool.

It's a complicated mix, calculated to beat a system it took back-boned animals millions of years to devise. Over the course of evolution, our bodies have come up with three methods to avoid bleeding to death: our blood vessels constrict, blood components called platelets huddle together to form a plug, and a network of fibers coagulate to reinforce the platelet plug. Chemicals in black-fly saliva defeat all three.

These chemicals have served blackflies extraordinarily well, but they could help us too. Cupp is now cloning cells from the insects' salivary glands, hoping to create new medicines to combat stroke and heart disease. His work could even yield a vaccine to help de-sensitize people to blackfly bites.

To deflect blackflies, people have smeared themselves with pine tar, pork fat and kerosene. Scientists have tried to kill off the larvae with some of the world's most noxious chemicals, poisoning rivers with everything from DDT to chlordane.

One reason for the ferocity of the human counterattack is that in parts of Africa and Latin America, some species of blackflies carry a parasite causing river blindness, a disease so common that in some villages, it blinds up to a third of wage-earning adults.

The most successful blackfly control method developed so far is a natural bacterium, discovered in 1977 from sand in the Negev desert, known as *Bacillus thuringienis* var. *israelensis,* or Bti for short. In liquid form, poured into rivers and streams, Bti kills blackfly larvae, mosquito larvae and almost nothing else. Bti does not seem to harm fish or the other aquatic creatures that eat blackfly larvae, and the predators seem to have no trouble finding other things to eat once the blackfly larvae are gone.

Bti is considered experimental. To use it requires a special permit from state fish and wildlife officials. If you have a small stream in your backyard, you can kill many blackfly larvae with a broom. Just sweep them away from their anchoring spots and they'll die.

To defend against the adults, folks use Avon's Skin-So-Soft (it repels most bugs) and products containing 100 percent DEET (unfortunately, although the bugs won't bite, they'll still hover). Entomologist John Burger recommends a wide-brimmed hat—it will deflect swarms descending from above. Serious gardeners might consider wearing the beekeepers' zippered veil over a wide-brimmed hat, preferably with a stiff brim.

Then, there's the option that turn-of-the-century Northwoods writer Stewart Edward White recommended: just squash them. "You just place your finger calmly and firmly on the spot. . . . In this is great, heartlifting joy," he promised. "It may be unholy joy, perhaps even vengeful, but it leaves the spirit ecstatic."

The Secret Lives
of Worms

🐛

THEY'LL BOIL UP FROM THE SOIL as you dig in the garden; they'll appear in country stores in little tubs in the refrigerator case—sometimes upsettingly near the cream cheese. Even if you don't fish or dig in the dirt, you're sure to see them on sidewalks and streets after a hard rain.

Earthworms are as sure a sign of spring as the robins who eat them. Yet the birds always get top billing. And that really isn't fair. True, earthworms may not be the world's handsomest animals. (Aristotle referred to them inelegantly as "earth's guts"—but he also thought earthworms formed by parthenogenesis and eventually became eels.) But no less an expert than Darwin championed earthworms: "It may be doubted whether there are many other animals which have played so important a part in the history of the world," he wrote in his book on the creatures in 1892.

Without earthworms' tunnels to oxygenate the soil and their feces, or castings, to enrich it, much of the Earth would be hard, cold and sterile. And earthworms have many other amiable qualities as well. "I like them," says Samuel James, "because they're toothless, nonviolent and easygoing." In fact, the Iowa professor likes them so much that he's made a career of studying these companionable, though slimy, invertebrates.

Earthworms make fine gardening partners, good pets for young children (they can live up to six years) and entertaining guests in the home or school terrarium (where they will also eat your garbage and turn it into top-grade compost). Earthworms are far more interesting, important, complex and mysterious than their pink, squashed forms on rainy sidewalks might suggest.

Few creatures are at their best after they've been stepped on (and alas, earthworms "have been getting stepped on ever since there were vertebrates to step on them," James says). But even dead, they're underestimated. "People think they're just mush inside, but they're not," says Ardis Johnston, an invertebrate zoologist at Harvard's Museum of Comparative Zoology. It's not as if earthworms have nothing between their ears. Actually they *don't* have ears, but they *do* have brains—and hearts with valves, and blood, and many of the organs that we do.

To really appreciate earthworms, you need to encounter them alive and well in their natural element—like in your garden. Earthworms spend the day literally eating their way through the organic matter of the soil. Their meals aren't random. They avoid eating their own castings, the world's best plant food. Sometimes they drag choice morsels, such as fallen leaves, into their burrows for later snacking. (Occasionally you'll even find a bird feather in there.)

Earthworms often construct their burrows under small rocks. (This is why flagstone footpaths tend to sink: worms are working beneath, moving the earth from below and piling it on the surface.) They line their tunnels with slime, which is one reason they can slip down them like greased lightning—so fast sometimes it's hard to keep up with them with a shovel. Once James hacked away at the earth for half an hour during a titanic struggle with a previously undescribed Puerto Rican species. (He estimates that, amazingly, perhaps more than 100 species of American earthworms are still undescribed! About 70 are known so far.) The scientist eventually won, and got out the 39-inch-long animal, albeit in three pieces.

Contrary to popular belief, cutting up a worm into pieces doesn't create extra worms. Many earthworms—especially darker species who live near the surface—can regenerate their tail ends, but their tails can't grow new heads. The Austrian ethologist Konrad Lorenz observed that most worm-eating creatures seem to select the worm's tail end, but this may in fact reflect the worm's preference instead.

If you have hold of one end of a fleeing earthworm, you'll marvel at its strength as it pulls down into its burrow. Earthworms use tiny hairs called setae and two kinds of muscles to move. "Like the claws of a cat," as Mary Appelhof puts it in her book *Worms Eat My Garbage*, these hairs can extend or retract and act as brakes. The stiff setae push against a surface to keep that portion of the worm from moving while the muscles contract. Short muscles circling the worm's body tighten to make the worm long and thin. Lengthwise muscles pull the segments of the worm closer together, causing the worm to shorten and swell. It's in this position that worms are most easily picked up—but you need to be quick at it, because they're soon off and tunneling again.

Earthworms know that strong light and being touched are bad signs, usually indicating something is coming to eat them. Even though they don't have eyes, they can detect light with special cells located all over their bodies. Though they don't have noses or tongues, they have thousands of chemical receptors—as many as 700 per square millimeter of worm.

Oddly, if a worm is near the surface, its response to danger is to come up to escape. In Florida, bait collectors—"worm grunters" as they are sometimes referred to—"call up" worms by pounding a wooden stake into the ground and then rubbing a coarse piece of wood across it; in Missouri, professional grunters use gas-powered soil tampers.

You may not need to dig or grunt to find worms in the spring. If you walk softly, you'll see some species of worms—nightcrawlers—out of their burrows on your lawn in the early morning or evening. This time of year, they emerge from the earth at night and make love in the wet, green grass.

Earthworms copulate as we do—sort of. They mate belly to belly, but (literally) with a twist: head to tail. (How can you tell? The band of swollen tissue on a mature worm, the clitellum, is located more toward the front half.) Because earthworms are hermaphrodites, what both partners are doing is swapping sperm. They'll be at it for up to three hours, joined by two bands of slime emitted by each partner's clitellum. A few days later, each worm will lay its eggs in a cocoon constructed of hardening slime. You'll encounter these lemon-shaped, yellowish cocoons as you garden.

Unfortunately, most folks' longest looks at earthworms happen on sidewalks and streets when spring rains flood the worms' burrows. Most of these poor creatures are about to be drowned, fried or smooshed. (The ultraviolet rays of the sun are worms' worst enemies, according to James: "They need SPF 30 or 40 just to stay alive," he says.)

"These exposed, pink, hustling worms are truly needy," writes Doris Gove in an essay titled "Something You Can Do if You Don't Have Time to Patch the Ozone Hole." So what can one person do? "Help them," exhorts the essayist. If this is a mass evacuation, suggests James, you might want to lift them (not stab them) with a plastic fork. Place each worm three to four feet back from the pavement, so they won't wander out again. And if people stare, Gove has two suggestions: a) invite them to help, or b) talk to the worm as you pick it up.

Birds' Nests

"The Heart-Breaking Solemnity of Eggs"

꧁

ETH RUESS was planning to change the floral garland above her front door one April. But decorating taste was overridden by needs more primal: when she prepared to take down the old garland, she discovered that a pair of soft gray eastern phoebes had claimed it as a base for a mud and grass nest.

"I had been wondering, do these roses look real?" Ruess said. But after the four white eggs hatched and the fledglings flew away, she had her answer: "I guess they do!"

This time of year, you'll see birds nesting almost everywhere: least terns and piping plovers directly on beach sand, wood ducks in abandoned woodpecker holes, robins in apple trees and under house eaves. And in stick-pile nests so flimsy you can look up through the bottom to see the eggs, great blue herons are raising nestlings 40 feet off the ground over swamps.

Some of the sites birds choose seem to defy reason. House wrens have nested in the pockets of scarecrows, in tin cans and in the rear axle of a car that was actually driven (the eggs hatched!). Maine Audubon's Robert Hooper recently went to launch the Society's canoe and found that in the week since he'd last used it, a phoebe had built a nest in the overturned craft's center thwart.

New Hampshire naturalist Neal Clark reports a pair of killdeer—robin-sized plovers that often nest in fields and pastures— chose to nest on the cobblestone steps of the Atomic Energy Commission headquarters in Washington, D.C. And the Santa Barbara Museum of Natural History in California once enshrined the nest of a long-gone black-chinned hummingbird who built her cup-shaped one-inch nest right on top of an orange.

"Birds really are visible much more than most mammals," notes Joan Dunning, who spent years observing birds at their nests for her book *Secrets of the Nest*. "Think how infrequently we see skunks, or rabbits," she points out. "If you wanted to see their nest, you might see a little hole. You don't know what's going on down there. But with birds, you can see what is happening."

Not only can you see what is happening, but often you can watch the entire process, from nest building to fledging, unfold within six weeks, right under your nose. Many species, including robins, house finches, barn swallows, house sparrows and phoebes, nest in window boxes, under eaves and in old Christmas wreaths— and they're not disturbed if you peek, or lift up your child for a view. "These species know what they're getting into," says Hooper. "They're pretty habituated to humans." Just don't touch the birds or their eggs, he advises, and don't look more than once or twice a day. Hold up a hand mirror to let you see into the nest.

The whole idea of nesting, Dunning considers, is quite astonishing if not downright absurd: "We have this funny little animal walking or hopping along on two feet, with its hands essentially tied behind its back, the survival of its species depending on how well it can protect and keep warm a ridiculous, round, rolly, fragile thing, containing its future offspring," she writes.

As part of the research for her book, Dunning tried caring for an egg on her kitchen floor, pushing it around with her nose. "I heard foxes in the living room, snakes in the broom closet, raccoons sneaking around in the cabinets behind the cereal boxes," she wrote.

The hen's dilemma, the fragility of the future, is the essence of what Frances Hodgson Burnett termed "the immense, tender, terrible, heart-breaking beauty and solemnity of Eggs. If there had been one person in that garden who had not known through all his or her innermost being if an Egg were taken away or hurt the whole world would whirl round and crash through space and come to an end," Burnett wrote in *The Secret Garden* " . . . there could have been no happiness even in that golden springtime air."

How to keep the egg safe?

One way birds solve the dilemma is to build nests from materials ranging from cellophane to lichens. Some bird lovers, along with seed and water, offer birds short (2- to 3-inch) lengths of yarn, bits of cloth, lint, even human and pet hair, which birds weave into their nests.

Many birds also visit mud puddles to gather pellets to strengthen the walls of their nests. Robins muddy their red breasts while rotating around their newly plastered nests to create smooth bowls. Warblers and hummingbirds pick at spider webs and tent caterpillar cocoons, gathering sticky gossamer to bind their nests to branches. Hummingbirds collect lichens to camouflage the outside of their walnut-size nests, and gather milkweed, feathers and fern down to make a soft lining for their two snowy eggs.

We tend to think of most nests as woven, bowl-shaped affairs, but many are not. Owls, bluebirds, titmice and wood ducks, for instance, nest in tree hollows (or nest boxes), for which they gather eclectic linings. (Titmice are particularly fond of shed snakeskins and will even pull hair from squirrels' tails, live woodchucks, even men's beards.) A few birds—such as puffins and burrowing owls—*dig* holes in which they raise their young, and the burrowing owls even line theirs with cow dung. Still others, including killdeer, terns and most ducks, lay eggs on the ground. Some birds, like red-eyed vireos, construct hammocklike nests suspended between the forks of twigs; others, including northern orioles, weave hanging, pendulous pouches that squeeze shut like a drawstring purse with the weight of parents and nestlings.

The brown-headed cowbird doesn't nest at all. It evolved on the prairies, eating the insects the thundering herds kicked up from the grass. Because its movements were tied to the wandering buffalo, the cowbird didn't have time to build a nest, incubate eggs and feed its fledgling young—so it solved the problem by laying its eggs in other birds' nests. Oddly, small songbirds like warblers and vireos don't seem to notice when one of "their" eggs hatches out a cow-bird mega-chick. The surrogate parents work slavishly to feed the interloper's child, usually at the expense of their own. The cost is high, because a female cowbird may lay up to eight eggs per year—each of which will destroy a whole nestful of baby birds of other species.

Even raising a normal-sized chick of the right species is a Herculean task. Dunning reports that robin parents feed each of their four nestlings three pounds of food in the two weeks between hatching and fledging—the equivalent of 14 feet of earthworms per chick per day. When you see a robin carrying off a worm, you can bet it's going to a nest. In fact, you may see robins doing this for months. That's because robins raise up to three clutches of eggs each spring.

"If you watch them, it adds another dimension to your life, the way art does," Dunning said. "It adds a layer of events around your observations—another network of life." And nothing beats watching the moment of first flight for drama, suspense and delight. For this is the promise of every bird nest: a new opportunity for youth to take wing.

Summer

Jellyfish

Jell-O with a Mouth

EACH SUMMER, Frank Steimle gets a lot of phone calls from beachgoers about jellyfish. What do the callers want? "They want us to *do* something about them," says the exasperated Steimle, a marine biologist at the National Marine Fisheries Service's Northeast Fisheries Center in New Jersey. "Like get rid of them."

But jellyfish are impossible to evict. Unlike sharks, you can't exclude them from bathing areas with nets. Parts of the gelatinous creatures would simply slosh through, each piece of jellyfish puree as capable of stinging as the whole.

Killing them won't protect you: the really notorious species can still deliver a sting after drying up on the beach.

Don't blame the jellies. They couldn't swim away even if they wanted to. "They move by pulsing around, but they can't really swim," says Sarah Jordan, who has reared hundreds of them for Boston's New England Aquarium.

Jellyfish are mostly deep-sea animals. Their movements are largely at the mercy of ocean currents, so coming to shore isn't their idea. In fact, jellyfish probably have very few ideas, since they don't have brains. They don't even have heads.

For a creature so feared, jellies are rather helpless. They have no organs. They have no blood. They have no eyes. They regenerate lost body parts easily because there's so little to regenerate—they're 95 percent water. "Jell-O with a mouth," as one scientist puts it.

Still, what little they do have has done the job quite nicely for the

past 500 million years: a simple nerve network and primitive muscles allow them to pulse through the water. The bell-shaped mantle is fringed with tentacles, and a cluster of longer structures hangs
down from the center like the handle of an umbrella. These, believe it or not, are the jellyfish's *lips*.

Most portions of the jellyfish, but particularly the tentacles, are
endowed with stinging, harpoonlike cells that burst out of the crit-
ter whenever it brushes against something. The tentacles of some
types of jellyfish are designed to stun and capture prey so small that
human skin is too thick to even feel the sting. But several jellyfish do
sting people, and generally people are against this. Public fear is so
great that, in 1966, Congress passed the Jellyfish Control Act, ap-
propriating $5 million to find ways to "control and eliminate jelly-
fish and other such pests in our coastal waters."

Good thing the money ran out. As it so happens, the oceans'
more than 2,000 species of jellylike, see-through creatures may be
some of the most important players in the health of the world's waters. They provide food for some species (sea turtles and giant ocean
sunfish eat them almost exclusively). They offer shelter to others
(young cod and haddock, among others, hide behind jellies' cur-
tain of stinging tentacles). And their appetites regulate the number
of their prey species, from tiny plankton to other jellyfish and jellyfish look-alikes.

The jellyfish you are most likely to bump into while you're
swimming near the shore won't hurt you. Among the commonest
species is the moon jelly, a milky white animal with a bold cloverleaf design on its top, a creature so benign you can hold it in your
hand. (While you're examining it, note the color of the cloverleaf:
if white, you've got a female; if pink, a male.)

In fact, jellyfish and their gelatinous relatives do us far more
good than harm. They're even helping researchers investigate basic
questions about biology.

"People are very confused about jellyfish," says Wendy Lull,
director of New Hampshire's Seacoast Science Center. No wonder.
Many jellyfish aren't actually jellyfish after all. The commonest

gelatinous animals in the ocean—the small glistening globs you find washed up on the beach—are not jellyfish but ctenophores (pronounced TEE-no-fors), sometimes also called comb jellies. They don't have stinging cells. They use sticky drool to capture fish fry, invertebrates and other ctenophores. They don't move by pulsing, but by wiggling hairlike structures called cilia, which look like the teeth of a comb. (Ctenophores have the largest cilia of any creatures in the world, which makes them of great interest to Sidney Tamm; his studies at the Marine Biological Laboratory in Massachusetts may help explain how cilia keep lungs clear, propel sperm and perform many other critical functions.)

But ctenophores' most spectacular trick—as you'll see if you swim on a night when they mass near the shore—is that when jostled, they glow.

The flashes may scare off predators; no one's sure. But at least we know how, if not why, ctenophores and certain other jellyfish glow: Andrew Miller, another scientist at Marine Biological Laboratory, explains that ctenophores possess a protein, aequorin, in special capsules in the mantle. When the animals release calcium into the capsules, a glow results.

Miller is using aequorin in the laboratory as a biological marker, allowing him to watch how calcium moves within cells in order to understand basic biological processes. But West Coast Native American tribes recognized this property long ago. They dried ctenophores and certain jellyfish to a powder, and applied it to their bodies during ceremonial nighttime dances. As the dancers sweated with exertion, the calcium in their perspiration would react with the protein, causing the dancers to glow green in the firelight.

If the most beautiful jellyfish isn't really a jellyfish, neither, technically, is the most dreaded. The Portuguese man-of-war, mainly a tropical, deep-sea species, is actually a creature called a hydrozoan. This powerful stinger is easily recognized: first you'll spot its brilliant blue, pink or purple sail, allowing it to ride the wind. Below the sail is the creature's gas-filled float, and beneath it, the 40- to 50-foot-long tentacles. Each man-of-war is actually a colony of individuals, some responsible for capturing food, some for reproduction, others for eating.

One reason jellyfish and their relatives are so confusing is that they are difficult to study. They start out virtually invisible and end up see-through. Young jellyfish-to-be spend the winter as shy polyps, sea-anemone-like blobs less than a quarter-inch long, often hiding in the cracks on jetty pilings. Then, depending on the species, they may go through several other stages, during which they may look like a stack of tiny pancakes made of Jell-O, or floating stars, until finally they turn into proper-looking jellyfish.

Events during any of these stages might affect jellyfish numbers and whether or not they are coming to a beach near you, explains Barbara Sullivan, a marine research scientist at the University of Rhode Island. She's investigating the movements and foods of the lion's mane jellyfish, the stinging, rust-colored beings who alarmed East Coast beachgoers with their sudden "blooms" in 1992, 1987 and 1986. And they're not the only jellies that "bloom." Sometimes, around the Chesapeake, the stinging nettle infests bays and estuaries so thickly it clogs fishermen's nets.

Even during bloom years, we have it pretty easy in temperate North America. Australia has the sea wasp, whose dangerous sting is so painful its victims think they've been bitten by sharks. And in the Arctic, there's the lion's mane again, but this time it's a Hitchcock version of The Blob: there, the animal's mantle grows up to 8 feet across, and its tentacles stretch 200 feet. Frank Steimle is glad his callers haven't heard about those.

What should you do about close encounters of the gelatinous kind? Experts advise that if you see a jellyfish, unless you have a positive ID on a moon jelly or a ctenophore, assume it can sting you—even if it's dried up and dead on the beach. Don't touch it.

If a jellyfish is floating beside you in the water, don't panic. Just swim away calmly. (If you thrash off in a hurry, you might create waves that move the floating tentacles toward you.)

Like bee stings, jellyfish stings can produce violent reactions in allergic people, requiring emergency room treatment. But for most folks, these remedies will suffice:

• Flush the area with seawater—*not* fresh water. Fresh water will make the sting more painful.

• Apply a paste of meat tenderizer mixed in seawater (or vinegar). It dissolves the poison by breaking down its proteins.

• Don't try to remove the stingers; they're too small. You'll only further irritate the area. But sometimes a piece of tentacle will stick to you like seaweed. Carefully peel it off, using a towel to shield your hands.

Sex and the Single Dragonfly

A SUMMER DUSK: mist rises over the river as canoeists approach a bend. Making the turn, they are greeted with a startling sight: in the middle of the water rises what looks like a round, head-sized object, seemingly attached to a mysterious, cone-shaped lump stretching a foot or so long.

"People would nearly tip their canoes over," said Paul Miliotis, whose head and net alarmed people all evening that July night nine years ago. "I must have looked like the Creature from the Black Lagoon."

Lurking submerged up to his neck, the Texas-based naturalist was seeking quarry stranger than the horror film star he resembled: a rare, night-loving species of dragonfly that gathers just above the surface of the middle of certain rivers. But whether rare or common, North America's 500 or so dragonfly species surely number among the weirdest creatures on six legs, and among the most fearsome predators on four wings.

"They're monsters," says Virginia Carpenter, the Rhode Island-based author of *Dragonflies and Damselflies of Cape Cod*. These airborne predators' voracious appetites wipe out millions of mosquitoes, flies, midges—and even claim other dragonflies. "I once saw one carrying three other dragonflies half its size," Carpenter said. "Just spectacular."

"They're like alien beings," says Patrick McCarthy, an ecologist with The Nature Conservancy. His surveys pinpointed the northernmost breeding ponds of the rare banded bog skimmer and led to the Conservancy's purchase of the nation's first preserve for an endangered dragonfly—20 acres near Durham, New Hampshire.

Among the otherworldly abilities of dragonflies, McCarthy explains, is their method of childhood locomotion: as nymphs, or larvae, young dragonflies propel themselves though the water by jetting water out their tail ends. They also breathe through gills in this same, multi-use aperture. The nymph's other pole is just as strange: the front of the face is dominated by a giant, hook-covered, double-hinged lower lip, which it can shoot out at the speed of 0.03 of a second to capture water bugs, larvae and even small fish. (The nymph keeps its fabulous anus closed during this maneuver, so as not to trigger unwanted jet propulsion.)

After an average of two or three years as a nymph (although some nymphs may live up to 12 years), the dragonfly undergoes its alien metamorphosis, crawling up out of the water and then out of its own skin. James Needham of Cornell University could have been scripting a horror flick when he wrote in *A Manual of the Dragonflies of North America*: "First comes the splitting of the skin down the back and across the head, and the pushing up through the split of the head and thorax. The legs are slowly withdrawn from their sheaths . . . ." You may see the shed skin of the larvae resting on a rock or stem at the edge of a pond, lake or bog.

This time of year, at that same body of water, you're bound to see dragonflies engaged in what may be their strangest-looking activity: two flying together, The tail of one stuck firmly into the back of the other's head. And if you follow the same pair for a few minutes, you'll see more contortions: they'll form a sort of heart shape, one's tail still stuck to the head of the other, who in turn has curled a tail up to reach its companion's abdomen.

You're witnessing a chapter of the insect *Kama Sutra*—a sex act so athletic its voyeurs forget to blush. "One of the most bizarre performances to be seen anywhere," is how Harvard entomologist Howard Ensign Evans describes it in *Life on a Little-Known Planet*.

But considering the anatomical quandary these insects face, they seem to have arrived at an admirable solution. Male dragonflies have clasping organs at their tail end, which are supposed to fit into grooves at the back of the female's head. When he finds a female, the male flies above and slightly behind her. If she's receptive, she allows him to fasten his claspers to the grooves while the two fly together. All this is great, except for one problem: now his tail end, where his sex organs are, is occupied with her forward parts—far from the female opening males are normally so interested in.

Happily, the male dragonfly can swing his sex organs up toward a special pouch in his abdomen, right in back of his legs, and load it with sperm. (Male damselflies, dragonfly relatives whose wings don't lie flat like a biplane's but are angled like a fairy's, often do this after they have grasped the female. Many male dragonflies do it in advance.) This way the female can, if she chooses, loop her own abdomen up, touch her tail end to her mate's sperm-containing pouch and fertilize her eggs.

Some species complete this loop in flight; others perch high in a tree during the climax. Dragonfly couples may remain together for up to an hour. Often the male, the original Sensitive New Age Guy, accompanies the female as she lays her eggs, holding her by the neck as she backs down a stem into the water to deposit her eggs. Sometimes, as in the case of the white-tailed dragonfly (a big dark dragonfly with a white spot on the tail), the male releases his mate, but guides her to a clump of sticks or mud and hovers near while she lays her eggs beneath the surface.

Much of the dragonfly action you'll see at your local pond during summer is related to sex. Male dragonflies stake out territories to which they hope to attract mates. If you go to the same place, you're likely to see the same individuals patrolling day after day. (A Finnish study of one species of smallish dragonfly found males patrolled an area 7 to 13 feet wide, permitting no other males to enter.) Watch for their spiraling aerial combat: rival males chase one another in circles, all the while losing altitude. They'll spiral downward until the intruder leaves or they fight.

Dragonflies fight much like they hunt. With hairy legs extended, they grab the meal (or rival) and then bite with formidable jaws, all

AT SUMMER PONDS, MUCH OF A DRAGONFLY'S
ACTIVITY IS RELATED TO SEX, WITH MALES STAKING OUT
TERRITORIES TO WHICH THEY ATTRACT MATES.

in midair. But male dragonflies save fighting as a last resort, preferring to dangle, flutter and flash their colorful spots and iridescent
patches at one another in ritualized threat displays.

It's a wise strategy. Few creatures survive attack by a dragonfly,
for it seldom misses its mark. Eyes occupy about three-quarters of a
dragonfly's face. Thousands of individual lenses in each eye—28,000
for the larger dragonflies—include a set near the top of the eye for
watching for predators above, a set for straight-ahead vision and a
magnifying set in the bottom third of the eye, for close-up views.

The design of the dragonfly's wing is older than the dinosaurs.
Laboratory measurements show their primitive wings can beat only
30 times per second, while a honeybee's can hit 250, and certain
midges more than 1,000. But the dragonfly can, and does, catch
them both. How? Aeronautical engineers at NASA, the Air Force
and the Navy have flown dragonflies through windtunnels and
hooked them to strength meters to figure out the secrets of their
speed and maneuverability. It turns out that by moving their two sets
of wings in opposite directions, dragonflies create powerful whirl-
winds to create three times more lift for their weight than the most
efficient of human designs.

The maneuverability that makes them such formidable predators helps them elude scientists' nets. But Miliotis, who houses his
extensive dragonfly collection at Harvard's Museum of Comparative
Zoology, is game: he likes "the physical challenge of playing a game
with an insect whose reflexes are five times better than yours. It's
kind of humbling.

"These things don't live lives like we do," he continues. "But the
more you watch them, the more you fall in love with them. They're
beautiful, they're amazing in flight, they're incredibly complex." He
likens dragonflies to birds of prey like falcons—after all, both pur-
sue lightning-quick prey on the wing, a feat requiring both speed and
skill. "You get to have immense respect for them."

Herring Gulls

Flying Beachcombers of Summer

❧

AT THE SHORE, it seems, they're everywhere: sidling up to your beach towel to steal your French fries, following your ferry boat like a pack of journalists after a jogging president, swirling out of the hazy blue sky like a summer snowstorm of white wings.

"The beach is simply unthinkable without these ever-present fellow-beachcombers," wrote Nobel-prizewinning naturalist Niko Tinbergen, who grew up watching herring gulls on Holland's North Sea shores.

It's hard to believe that herring gulls were rare on American beaches at the turn of the century. So popular were gull feathers in the millinery trade that dealers paid 40 cents for each bird shot. On one bridge between Boston and Cambridge, as Neal Clark tells us in his guide to avian invaders, *Birds on the Move*, officials stopped the shooting only because horses bolted at the gunfire.

Legal protection—and open-pit dumps—helped the gulls stage a spectacular comeback. Too spectacular, some say; now even many conservationists, worried about gulls' depredations on the nests of other shorebirds, think there may be too many of them.

White with a gray back, black wing tips and yellow beak, the herring gull is the DC-3 of "sea gulls." If you're looking at a gull, it's probably a herring gull. (Those brownish-white gulls are herring gulls, too—youngsters who start out life brown and become paler until they reach snowy maturity at age four.)

Because of their thieving and scavenging, a friend considers gulls "rats with wings" (he calls pigeons "living bus exhaust"). But to their many fans, herring gulls' success is part of their charm. Herring gulls steal our affection; we admire their very gall. Watching these agile, expressive birds can prove addictive once you begin to appreciate some of the capers these heroic villains pull off.

Herring gulls' biggest fan may be Nantucket journalist A.B.C. Whipple. He has pushed for the herring gull to replace the bald eagle as our national bird—admittedly a quixotic quest rivaling Ben Franklin's attempt to install turkeys on the backs of our quarters. But here's his reasoning: "If there is a nonendangered species in the United States today," he told author Clark, "it has to be the sea gull. They've learned to live from the detritus of our society."

Often, herring gulls don't wait for our stuff to become detritus before they eat it. Sometimes they'll steal a sandwich right out of your hand. People aren't the only victims of their robberies. They also steal food from other birds and even eat their eggs and young. (Occasionally, even other herring gulls make it onto the menu.)

Watching the getaways from their heists reveals their admirable aerial skills. At Yorkshire, England, A. Hazelwood described the theft of a Guillemot's egg: "While flying away with the egg in its bill, (the Herring Gull) was beset by another Herring Gull, which so pestered it that it released its booty," he wrote in the journal *British Birds*. "The second gull immediately stalled (in flight) and with a rapid maneuver, seized the egg by its pointed end as it fell and flew off with it." The whole episode took place in a vertical distance of about 50 feet, and the egg never broke—until the second gull consumed it.

Although gulls steal and scavenge, they also hunt live prey. When favorable winds create an updraft, the birds may hang motionless in the air above rabbit holes, waiting to dive as soon as a rabbit appears at the entrance. They also hunt moles. (While some people have seen herring gulls carrying off rats and even cats, it's almost certain the birds didn't kill them; they probably pick them up already dead at the dump, the way we get steak at the market.)

Most often, though, you'll see herring gulls feeding while walking along the edge of the water. (As boys, Tinbergen and his friends learned to follow the gulls to lead them to the day's motherlode of washed-up sea creatures: starfish, crabs, sometimes a dead seal or whale.) Quite often they pick up mollusks, whose hard shells they can't crack with their bills. This doesn't deter the crafty gulls: to crack them open, the birds carry clams, whelks and other shellfish in their beaks, fly over a hard surface, then drop them from a height.

The ornithologist B.B. Beck studied shell dropping by herring gulls on Cape Cod and discovered they had worked out a regular system. The birds found the clams at low tide and carried them to rocky areas, sea walls and paved roads or parking areas for distances of 100 to more than 600 feet. They usually flew low over the beaches, so that they could not see their target until they were just approaching it—indicating the birds had learned and remembered where the best drop sites were. In one area, 90 percent of the drops were directed at a particular sea wall, which occupied only 1 percent of the land the gulls overflew.

This penchant for dropping hard objects from heights can prove hazardous for those below. One winter, West London factory officials suspected sabotage when employees discovered skylights and windows regularly broken by nuts, bolts and bits of scrap iron. The culprits, it was discovered, were gulls.

In the fall of 1984, at the Smith and Wesson Company's golf driving range in Springfield, Massachusetts, herring gulls bombarded stunned employees with many-colored golf balls. The birds swiped an estimated 500 balls and dropped them around the neighborhood before company officials closed the range in exasperation.

For this reason, and for their habit of fearlessly defending their nests with sharp beaks, many scientists who have studied herring gulls include hard hats in their wardrobe of field clothes. Thanks to this courageous work, we beachgoers can now decode some of what herring gulls have been so loudly saying: "Gagagagaga. Gagagaga" means the bird has been alarmed by a predator. Then there's "Ow, ow, ow. Kee kee kee. Kyowkyowkyow": a long call, done with head arched forward, then moved under breast, then tossed upward, reserved for courtship and aggressive encounters, usually near their nesting grounds on secluded islands. Of course there's "kleew, kleew, kleew, kleew," the typical call of the gull heard throughout the year. But what does it mean? Scientists haven't got a kleew.

Which is all the more reason for you to watch these creatures closely this summer. Maybe you'll figure it out. Even if not, you'll be in good company. For Niko Tinbergen, studying these common, graceful, adaptable birds offered unending delight. "I derived a vague but intense satisfaction from just being with the gulls," he wrote in his classic field study, *The Herring Gull's World*, ". . . watching the snow-white birds soaring up in the blue sky, and assuming, or rather knowing, that they were feeling just as happy as I was."

Going for the Gold

&

THIRTY YEARS AGO, Ernest Foley was living on Long Island with his wife and daughter and happily running an auto body shop. Then one day he read an 1866 geological survey. It said there was gold to be found up north. There was a map showing the river where the gold was. So Foley drove north. He found the river. And he found gold.

"In this day and age, most people believe that all of the gold in the United States had already been discovered during the early Gold Rush days," Foley wrote. "That, of course," he learned, "is pure bunk."

Foley and his family moved and built a home near the banks of the river called the Wild Ammonoosuc. He never got rich, but he achieved a fame of sorts: until his death a few years back, he was known as The Old Prospector and as the author of a booklet that has sold thousands: "How to Find and Pan Gold in New England."

Gold! In New England?

If there's gold in New England, then there must be gold just about everywhere.

Which there is.

Not necessarily enough to get rich on, mind you. But enough to make for an entertaining summer outing.

Still unconvinced? At first, George Streeter didn't believe it, either. When people started coming into his metal detector shop in Keene, New Hampshire, asking for gold pans, he thought they were crazy. "I thought, there is no gold here," he says. "But there is!"

There's enough gold that Streeter, now an active member of one of the several New England gold-hunting clubs, offers a full line of gold-panning, mining and dredging supplies at Streeter's Treasure Hunting Supplies.

And there's enough gold that, if you pick the right spot on a lucky summer afternoon, you could well go home with at least a few flecks, no matter where you live.

"Gold! It's totally different from anything else," says Joseph Sinnott, a consulting geologist who was Massachusetts' state geologist for 22 years.

Gold is an element, which means it started out as itself at the dawn of the Earth. Gold is rare: the Earth's crust, it is estimated, is 0.001 parts per billion gold; the sea is a bit denser with gold, 0.004 parts per billion.

For its beauty, shine and rarity, gold has fascinated people since the Stone Age. Although so soft you can pound it three-millionths of an inch thin, gold does not corrode; gold coins fetched from sunken treasure ships after centuries underwater emerge as sparkling as new.

But perhaps gold's greatest difference from other precious metals lies in the way it fires human appetites. "If people see anything associated with gold," says Sinnott, "people have a tendency to chase it. Gold fever takes over."

After the California Gold Rush of 1848, the other side of the country experienced its own mini gold rush of sorts. In the 1860s, a fellow from Plymouth, Vermont, found a fat gold nugget under a rock in Buffalo Brook in Tyson. At least five gold mines opened up in northern New Hampshire, and at least two in Massachusetts. Those mines closed down—the two in Massachusetts evidently without ever finding any gold—but still folks quietly panned rivers and streams.

In fact, during the Great Depression, lots of folks panned gold from their local streams in order to afford groceries. At least that's what Willie Ford says, and he should know: "I was one of them."

Ford used to be a Maine lobsterman, but now, at 69, he's a full-time prospector living in Charlestown, New Hampshire. His skills are so well known that, a few years back, Norwegian American

Cruise lines gave him and his wife, Susanne, a free trip to Alaska so they could lecture on gold prospecting aboard the five-star cruise ship *Sagafjord.*

Prospecting in your local stream is a different matter from yanking nuggets from the Klondike. In the Northeast, you're most likely to find flakes and dust in rivers, known as placer gold. No one really knows where it came from. Some folks think the gold is from undiscovered veins in nearby mountains; it may have come down from glaciers. One thing's for sure: if you want to find it, you're going to spend hours standing in a river—which is a pretty nice place to be on a hot summer day.

Because gold is the second densest element—it's twice as heavy as lead and six times heavier than most rock—it tends to concentrate in stream beds and banks. Spring floods sweep the gold along until it comes to an obstruction. Look at the back of a big boulder downstream.

Gold settles into cracks and crevices. A good place to check is among rocks where the river widens, allowing the current to slacken. Just about any place you could find a fat brook trout is a good spot to look for gold. A clue that you could be on the right track is the presence of heavy black sand known as magnetite (so called because you can pick it up with a magnet).

You can recover river gold using a pan, sluice or dredge. All work on the same basic principle: slosh water around with your gravel and eventually, because gold is so heavy, gold will be the last thing left in the bottom.

Each method has its champions. Ford uses a dredge, a gas-powered centrifugal pump that sucks up gravel and water and passes it through a sluice box, a large-holed grate.

But Foley called the gold pan, alone, "man's finest tool for the recovery of gold in placer mining." It's simple. It's cheap (it costs about $10—or just use your cast-iron skillet, like many forty-niners did). And to pan for gold, you don't need a permit (which you do for dredges and sluices, at least in some states).

You may find plenty of other interesting items in your pan as well. Areas known for gold also often yield garnets. You may also find diamonds. Minerals often mistaken for gold include iron pyrite ("fool's gold"), chalcopyrite and yellow mica. To test your find, press it between two rocks; if it crushes to a powder, it's iron pyrite or chalcopyrite. If it floats on the surface, it's yellow mica.

If it can be cut with a knife or flattened by pounding, if it sinks to the bottom of the pan, it's gold.

"People see it in their pan once and they're hooked," says Ford. "But if they keep it for a recreation, they'll be fine, and have a good time. No one should ever, ever go out there with the idea of getting rich."

Bats

Nighttime's Aerial Show

🐝

WHEN THE POET RUTH PITCHER discovered a bat in her house and picked it up, she found it "warm as milk, soft as a flower, smooth as silk"—but alas, seldom do homeowners react to a bat in the house with an outpouring of poetry.

Instead, too many folks go to the closet to get the broom. But if you simply turn off the lights, open a window and watch the bat fly away into the night, the sight will certainly repay your courtesy: you may be in for an evening of aerial entertainment rivaling the Navy's Blue Angels, shaming the most daring circus aerialists.

Consider this maneuver, which one bat-watcher observed right outside a third-story hotel window: "The bat would be as much as two feet above the mosquito, but on approaching it would instantly arrest its flight, turning what appeared to be a complete somersault, but righting itself almost the same instant. When flying below the mosquito, it seemed to have the facility of gyrating upwards, its movement executed with incredible rapidity . . . ."

These are the words of the late Charles Campbell, a malaria expert who admired bats so much he built several 60-foot-tall shingled bat houses in the 1920s to attract them. To say he "enjoyed" watching bats fly is too tame a word; in his 1925 book *Bats, Mosquitoes and Dollars,* he described his feelings as "frenzied ecstasy."

When it comes to bats, that's a feeling Thomas Kunz understands. "It's easy to fall in love with them," he says—and he should know. This Boston University biology professor estimates he has personally handled 100,000 of them during his more than 20 years of work with bats around the world. "They're beautiful little animals," he says, "wonderful to watch."

August is the best time for bat watching—both outside and, occasionally, inside your house. That's because young bats are flying now (sometimes misguidedly into your living quarters). Born in June and July, baby bats strengthen their pectoral muscles by doing upside-down push-ups (push-downs?) from the ceiling of the barn or attic where they were born; then they take their first test-flights inside their nursery. Now they're ready to join the adults in the skies.

Watch for bats just before dark. They'll emerge around 7:30 to 8:30 P.M. "In the suburbs, just about every backyard has a bat or two flying around at night," Kunz says.

If there are no bats in your yard, look for them over any body of water, or at a nighttime ball game (you'll see them chasing moths around the lights).

The continental United States hosts 42 species of bats. What species are you seeing? If they're big and brown, they're probably big brown bats. If they're little and brown, they're probably little brown bats. No kidding—bats are sensibly named. These two are among the most common. Things get a bit more complicated if you live in Texas, the state that boasts, among other things, more bat species—32—than any other. And if you're anywhere near Braken Cave in Central Texas around dusk, you're probably seeing Mexican free-tailed bats—20 million of them boil out of the cave each evening, the largest surviving bat colony in the world.

If you live in more northerly climes, however, and in the country, you're most likely to see little brown bats. Hundreds of them—mothers and youngsters—may emerge from a barn or an attic in one night. (Most males roost singly in the summers, and you might find one sleeping behind a shutter.) Big brown bats, with thumb-sized bodies and wings spanning up to 14 inches, are more common in cities.

Kunz estimates that 50,000 bats summer in any given 100-square-mile area of his native New England. Those bats who live within the Boston area's Route 128 alone eat an estimated 13 tons of bugs each summer. (In the North, most bats migrate to hibernate in caves and mines. Some, though, hibernate in houses.)

One great way to watch bats hunt is to toss a small pebble in the air near a flying bat. If your aim is good, the bat will immediately sense it and wheel, midair, to power-dive toward the stone. This is a great game to play with your kids. It's almost like flying the bat like a kite.

If your pebble were really a meal, the bat would use its wings— and sometimes its tail membranes—as a sort of net to catch it in, then tuck its head to eat it. But the bat, of course, won't be fooled by your pebble for long, because these insect-eating bats (and some fruit-eating bats too) use sonar.

Emitting high-pitched sounds we can't hear and listening for the returning echoes, bats catch about half of the insects they chase. This is a success rate far superior to most predators. Bengal tigers, for example, catch only one out of every five of their intended meals.

A bat's efficiency is all the more amazing when you consider that some of its would-be meals have developed slick countermeasures. Some moths, upon detecting a bat's approach, emit high-pitched clicks that interfere with the bat's sonar. Others mimic a sound produced by unsavory moths. And still others evade the bat by looping erratically in the air; if that fails, the moth will fold its wings and dive to the ground. If you watch a bat hunting moths near a street lamp, you may be able to see this.

Between midnight and 4 A.M., most bats take a break from hunting and "hang up" at their home away from home—like a convenient ledge in a car port, cavities inside buildings, in park shelters or stairwells, located somewhere between their sleeping roosts and their hunting grounds. If, by day, you find bat guano and moth wings on the ground and look up and don't see any bats, you've probably discovered a roost to which groups of bats will return every night.

Here you can watch small clusters of bats hanging upside down,

BATS USE SONAR TO HUNT FOR INSECTS AND CATCH
ABOUT HALF OF WHAT THEY CHASE—A SUCCESS RATE FAR
SUPERIOR TO THAT OF MOST PREDATORS.

fully awake, digesting their food, grooming their fur and communing with roostmates. Watch them use their thumbs like a Q-tip: they'll wet this innermost clawlike finger in their mouths, then whirl it around inside their ears to clean them. Bats will jockey with one another for position, elbowing each other out of the way, sometimes with audible vocal accompaniment.

Bats not only use their voices to hunt, but also to express their feelings: the mammalogist Ernest P. Walker, who kept a big brown bat in his Washington, D.C., laboratory, reported it purred when contented.

"Bats are beyond doubt the most maligned and misunderstood creatures on Earth," says Texas bat expert Merlin Tuttle. Largely out of ignorant fear, people have killed so many bats and destroyed so much bat habitat that 40 percent of the world's species of bats are now in danger of going extinct. Spearheading efforts to save bats worldwide, Tuttle founded Bat Conservation International in Austin, Texas. Part of its mission is to counter anti-bat propaganda with the real facts about bats.

Bats don't get in your hair. You're more likely to get a walrus in your hair than a bat. With its sonar, a bat can easily detect and avoid even a single strand of human hair.

Bats don't want to bite you. Many photos of bats show the bat grimacing horribly with mouth open, baring dozens of little pointed teeth. That's because the bat is being held captive by a monster 1,000 times its size, and like any intelligent mammal in that predicament, it's screaming its head off. In the hairy fist of King Kong, Fay Wray had it great compared to that bat.

No North American bats are vampires. Of the world's more than 900 species of bats, only 3 eat blood—and they live in South and Central America.

And unless you find a rabid bat (less than ½ of 1 percent of all bats, according to one study) and make it bite you, bats can't give you rabies. Unlike rabid dogs, rabid bats do not attack people. The strain of rabies currently plaguing the East Coast is carried by raccoons, not by bats.

One more thing. Bats don't come out of hell. They often come out of churches, though, where they like to roost in attics, which is appropriate: arguably, bats are the closest thing we've got to real angels. They're the only mammals that truly fly. And no one who hates mosquitoes can deny that bats are a godsend. A single bat is said to be able to eat 600 mosquito-sized bugs in one night.

SELECTED BIBLIOGRAPHY

MAMMALS

Campbell, Charles. *Bats, Mosquitoes, and Dollars.* Boston: The Stratford Company, 1925.

Rockwell, David. *Giving Voice to Bear.* Niwot, CO: Roberts Rinehart Publishers, 1991.

Rue, Leonard Lee III. *The World of the Red Fox.* Philadelphia: J.B. Lippincott Co, 1969.

Thomas, Elizabeth Marshall. *The Tribe of Tiger: Cats and Their Culture.* New York: Simon and Schuster, 1994.

Tuttle, Merlin. *America's Neighborhood Bats.* Austin: University of Texas Press, 1988.

Wells-Gosling, Nancy. *Flying Squirrels: Gliders in the Dark.* Washington, D.C.: Smithsonian Institution Press, 1985.

PLANTS

Ahmadjian, Vernon. *The Lichen Symbiosis.* New York: Wiley, 1993.

Embertson, Jane. *Pods: Wildflowers and Weeds in Their Final Beauty.* New York: Charles Scribners Sons, 1979.

Felt, Ephriam Porter. *Key to American Insect Galls.* Albany: University of New York State Museum, 1917.

Gibbons, Euell. *Stalking the Wild Asparagus.* New York: Van Rees Press, 1962.

Going, Maud. *With the Trees.* New York: Baker and Taylor, 1905.

Lemmon, Robert S. *The Best Loved Trees of America.* Garden City, NY: The American Garden Guild and Doubleday, 1946.

Peattie, Donald Culross. *A Natural History of Trees of East and Central North America*. New York: Bonanza Books, 1966.

Petrides, George A. *Eastern Trees*. Boston: Houghton Mifflin, 1988.

Richardson, David H. *Pollution Monitoring with Lichens*. Slough, England: Richmond Publishing Co., 1992.

INVERTEBRATES

Appelhof, Mary. *Worms Eat My Garbage*. Kalamazoo, MI: Flower Press, 1982.

Carpenter, Virginia. *Dragonflies and Damselflies of Cape Cod*. Brewster, MA: Cape Cod Museum of Natural History, 1991.

Dethier, Vincent. *Crickets and Katydids, Concerts and Solos*. Cambridge: Harvard University Press, 1992.

Evans, Howard Ensign. *Life on a Little-Known Planet*. New York: Dell, 1966.

Fabre, J. Henri. *The Insect World of J. Henri Fabre*. Boston: Beacon Press, 1991.

Hubbell, Sue. *Broadsides from the Other Orders*. New York: Random House, 1993.

Knott, Robert C. *Earthworms: A Teacher's Guide*. Berkeley, CA: Lawrence Hall of Science, University of California, 1991.

Needham, James. *A Manual of the Dragonflies of North America*. Berkeley, CA: University of California Press, 1955.

BIRDS

Clark, Neal. *Birds on the Move: A Guide to New England's Avian Invaders*. Unity, ME: North Country Press, 1988.

Dunning, Joan. *Secrets of the Nest*. Boston: Houghton Mifflin, 1994.

Eiserer, Len. *The American Robin*. Chicago: Nelson-Hall, 1976.

Forbush, Edward Howe. *A Natural History of American Birds*. Boston: Houghton Mifflin, 1925.

Martin, Alfred. *Hand Taming Wild Birds at the Feeder*. Freeport, ME: Bond Wheelwright Co., 1963.

Nero, Robert W. *The Great Grey Owl.* Washington, D.C.: Smithsonian Institution Press, 1987.

Peterson, Roger Tory. *Birds Over America.* New York: Dodd, Mead & Co., 1964.

Sutton, Patricia and Clay. *How to Spot an Owl.* Shelburne, VT: Chapters Publishing, 1994.

Voous, Karel. *Owls of the Northern Hemisphere.* Cambridge: MIT Press, 1989.

Wiberg, Hugh. *Hand-Feeding Wild Birds.* Norton, MA: Annedawn Publishing, 1993.

Tinbergen, Niko. *The Herring Gull's World.* New York: Lyons and Burford, 1989.

GEOLOGY, EARTH SCIENCES

Eckert, Alan W. *The Northeastern Quadrant.* New York: Harper and Row, 1987.

Johnson, Charles W. *Bogs of the Northeast.* Hanover, NH: University Press of New England, 1985.

Mottana, Annibale, Rodolfo Crespi and Guiseppe Liborio. *Guide to Rocks and Minerals.* New York: Simon and Schuster, 1978.

AQUATIC AND MARINE CREATURES

Carroll, David. *The Year of the Turtle: A Natural History.* Charlotte, VT: Camden House Publishing, 1991.

Carson, Rachel. *The Edge of the Sea.* Boston: Houghton Mifflin, 1979.

Sterling, Dorothy. *The Outer Lands.* New York: Norton, 1978.

NATURE GUIDES, FIELD GUIDES

Duensing, Edward and A.B. Millmoss. *The Backyard and Beyond.* Golden, CO: Fulcrum, 1992.

Duensing, Edward. *Talking to Fireflies, Shrinking the Moon: A Parent's Guide to Nature Activities.* New York: NAL-Dutton, 1990.

The Peterson Field Guides. Boston: Houghton Mifflin.
The Stokes Nature Guides. Boston: Houghton Mifflin.

STORIES, ESSAYS AND EXPLICATION

Bates, Marston. *The Forest and the Sea.* New York: Alfred Knopf, 1960.

Beston, Henry. *The Outermost House.* New York: Viking Press, 1962.

Dalrymple, Byron W. *Ice Fishing for Everybody.* New York: Lantern Press, 1948.

Forsyth, Adrian. *A Natural History of Sex.* Shelburne, VT: Chapters Publishing, 1993.

McPhee, John. *The Pine Barrens.* New York: Farrar, Straus, Giroux, 1981.

Schueler, Donald. *Incident at Eagle Ranch: Predators as Prey in the American West.* Tucson: University of Arizona Press, 1991.

Thoreau, Henry David. *Thoreau: A Week on the Concord and Merrimack Rivers; Walden; The Maine Woods; Cape Cod.* New York: Library of America, 1985.

Thoreau, Henry David. *The Heart of Thoreau's Journals.* Boston: Houghton Mifflin, 1927.

Walters, Mark Jerome. *Courtship in the Animal Kingdom.* New York: Doubleday, 1988.

INDEX